STEP
Into It

STEP Into It

OVERCOMING TRIALS THAT LEAD TO PURPOSE

Anita Morris

This book is dedicated to my two heartbeats, my sons, Brandon and Jordon. Your presence in my life is a cherished gift. I love you.

To my late husband, Cecil Morris, for being my greatest supporter on earth, encouraging me to go after my dreams and try new things.

Contents

Part 1: The Storms

Part 2: Stand

Contents

Part 3: Trust

Part 4: Endure

Part 5: Proceed

Resources

Foreword

We live in a time of unparalleled change: an era in which innovation, adaptation, and seismic cultural shifts are happening more frequently and dramatically. Add the normal stressors of life to the mix, and so many of us are living "on our heels" by reacting to life instead of living it. It's difficult to overstate how unnerving this can be, but it's evident in the rising rates of anxiety and depression in our society.

By picking up this book, you have taken a first and very important STEP out of reactive living and into re-engaging the purpose you were created for. If you're in the middle of a crisis, you've just taken your first STEP in the direction of help. If you're grieving, you've just taken your first STEP in the direction of healing. And if you're losing faith, you've just taken your first STEP in the direction of hope.

Anita Morris experienced one of the hardest things a human being will experience, and I had the heart-wrenching honor of walking with her through that process and beyond as her pastor. I believed God would faithfully help her and her sons "walk through the valley of the shadow of death" and knew that the day would come when she would walk alongside others going through heartbreak and hopelessness. As I write this foreword, I praise God that she has exceeded even my high expectations for how she would STEP into recovery and give us such an incredibly valuable resource to share with an uncertain world.

The fact that you have this book in your hands is itself proof that Anita's plan works. Her storms were severe and the reasons for her to stop writing were daunting. But she persevered, one STEP at a time, and practiced what she preaches, giving us a way to find God's plan when our plans fall apart. By boldly being authentic with her life events, her reactions, and her responses, Anita empowers us in our own lives, and I hope you'll bless her by letting her know how this book has changed your story too.

I encourage you to let down your guard and let God lead you into this new chapter of life. One STEP at a time, you'll get exactly where God wants you to be, which is the best place to be!

Rev. Joel Plantinga

Lead Pastor, Desert Winds Community Church

Introduction

Every once in a while, life comes around and punches you in the face—really hard. At times it completely knocks you down. And that's okay. It's okay to get knocked down. But at some point, you have to get up. Getting up, however, isn't always a quick reaction, and it doesn't need to be. Getting up is an act of perseverance, of determination, of will, and of desire. It's a process, a journey that should be approached one day at a time, one step at a time, and one breath at a time.

Throughout my life, I've experienced a few trials that took me down. In those heartbreaking circumstances, I felt broken and unsure if I would ever be okay. I wondered if I could be happy, healthy, and whole again. The uncertainty about my future made me uncomfortable. Each time I was faced with a life trial, my sole focus and goal was to overcome. So that's what I did. I overcame the trials.

But in 2018, I went through the most devastating trial I've ever experienced in my life—and it knocked me down *hard*. This time, overcoming wasn't my goal. I simply wanted to survive. But early in the healing process, something amazing happened. I was awakened to the power of God's purpose in the midst of my trial. That shifted everything. I no longer wanted to simply survive; I wanted to thrive. I reminded myself that I was an ambassador for Christ, so I rose up and responded to the awakening.

I embraced the painful journey, gathering the treasures and golden nuggets along the way. As I allowed myself to be present, focusing on what was happening in and around me, another realization came into focus. A transformation was happening—one that would bring me out of the storm in better condition than I had been going in.

Now I have a new perspective on the trials of life. They don't come to destroy us. As sad and painful as my trials have been, God has used them to draw me closer to Him, and I've learned more about His grace. I'm more intentional now about how I show up in the world. I'm living, thriving, and walking in obedience to God's call on my life in the midst of the storm.

Are you facing a trial in your life? Maybe in the past, you've experienced a storm that still prevents you from moving forward. How are you dealing with that? Sometimes we go through trials feeling sorry for ourselves. We wonder if we'll ever be okay again. We blame other people for our response to the trial. Instead of dealing with the reality of what's happening, we try to escape the pain. Does any of this resonate with you?

Maybe you dive into your work as a way of distracting yourself from the reality of the situation. Perhaps you've used alcohol or other substances as coping mechanisms. Or maybe you've just given up. You want to feel like yourself again, but you don't know what to do or where to start. Maybe you're just feeling stuck. If that sounds familiar, I have wonderful news: it doesn't have to be this way.

I want to help you see the abundance that is hidden within the painful places. I want to take you on a journey with me, one where you can begin to write a new narrative for yourself. When you experience awakening to a new mindset, you will be amazed. As you begin to walk in the truth of who you are, you will no longer be guided by your circumstances. Rather, looking adversity in the face, you can step into the power that lies within you.

In the following pages of this book, I'll share with you how facing the trials of life has the power to help you STEP into God's purpose. I want you to believe that there's something greater on the other side of your trial. As I walk through my own journey of recovery and healing, after the greatest storm of my life, I've discovered four powers at work in the process. I refer to these powers as steps.

Within each step you will discover how engaging with that particular power of the journey will lead you into the next, culminating with the awakening of purpose, which further facilitates healing and intentional living.

The Four Steps are STAND, TRUST, ENDURE, and PROCEED.

The STAND step provides you with practical tools to become deeply rooted in Christ so that you will be able to stand in your faith during the trial.

The TRUST step helps you to look beyond the trial to a powerful source—the Sovereign God. When you are aware that there's hope, you'll be more inclined to hold on.

The ENDURE step demonstrates the importance of allowing yourself to go through the emotions, twists, and turns along the road that take your breath away. You'll see examples of how feelings of helplessness and hopelessness are transformed into strength and power.

Finally, the PROCEED step prepares you to move into action. As you stand, trust, and endure what is before you, at some point you will become aware that there is a road you must take in order for this journey to reveal its purpose. This is where you meet the power of obedience.

By the end of this journey, you will gain a deeper understanding about the purpose of your trials. When you make yourself available to the process of walking through the storm, you will discover that overcoming is your stairway into transformation.

There is purpose in your storm. If you will allow yourself to believe this truth, you'll see that, even in the midst of your trial, God has the power to bring out the beauty that lies within you. You were designed for God's purpose, and that purpose doesn't end with your trial. Perhaps the trial is your beginning. Are you ready for an awakening? Let's STEP into it!

Part 1

THE
STORMS

"I have told you these things,
so that in me you may have peace.
In this world you will have trouble.
But take heart! I have overcome the world."

(John 16:33)

Chapter 1

Building the Dream

I met my husband when I was twenty-six years old. At the time, I was working at an accounting firm in downtown Los Angeles, California, as an assistant during the day and attending school in the evening. On the day that I crossed paths with him, I was on vacation from work and decided to do some studying at the beach before heading to class. I took my books with me and spent some time reading in the sand before heading to the Venice Beach boardwalk. The boardwalk was always alive with people performing and showing off their talents, skating, dancing to lively music, shopping at the numerous venues, and experiencing various eateries.

As I walked along, smiling and enjoying the atmosphere, I spotted two tall, muscular, very handsome men coming in my direction—and I've always been attracted to tall men. As they approached, I hoped one of them would say something to me. I wasn't the type to go after men; I always allowed them to be the chasers. As they came closer, I could tell they were going to stop me because they were staring and making their way towards me. With anticipation, I made eye contact with them, pretending to be nonchalant.

They said hello and introduced themselves, and I did the same. We shared a few words with each other and that was it. I told them that I didn't visit the beach often and was just there to read before class. We said our goodbyes and parted ways.

Two days later, I went back to the beach to read before class. Walking the boardwalk again, who did I see coming in my direction? You've probably guessed it—the two L.A. City firemen whom I had just told two days earlier that I don't visit the beach often. My first thought was, "Oh my goodness! They're gonna think I'm a liar!" As we drew near, grinning, I just went for it and said, "Seriously, you guys, I really don't go to the beach often. I'm just here to read before class." We all laughed, and they invited me to hang out with them at the basketball courts. I said yes and thought to myself, "Oh my goodness! I get to hang out with these fine men?"

We took a seat on a bench at the courts and talked for a while, getting to know each other. We laughed and joked until I had to leave for class. One guy told the other, "Go ahead—get her number." Cecil Morris asked if he could keep in touch with me, and I said yes. I gave him my phone number and walked away smiling. I wanted to look back so badly, but I was too afraid—I knew they would be looking at me and I didn't want to seem desperate. I wanted to be cool about the fact that I had just given this tall, fine, hunk of a man my phone number.

After a couple of days, he finally called me. We talked and laughed, and I remember being so tickled by his phone voice. It was softer and didn't match that big, strong body. At the end of the conversation, he asked me out on a date, and I accepted the invitation.

Our first date was to a restaurant called Moonshadows on the beach along Pacific Coast Highway. Cecil showed up at my apartment looking like a tall drink of fine wine. He wore a Karl Kani denim suit with a nice pair of dress shoes. I remember his beautiful, thick eyebrows when I opened the door. Lord knows I wanted to scream out and say, "*Dang, you're fine!*" I kept my cool, but on the inside I was screaming—he'd told me the dress code was casual! It had been a long day at work and I really didn't feel like going out, but I didn't want to cancel on him. So when he said to dress casual, I was happy enough to just throw on a pair of blue jeans and grab a green camouflage denim jacket. I didn't put much effort into making myself look amazing at all.

Nevertheless, we had a great time at dinner, with good conversation and lots of laughter. It was then that I really took notice of his laugh. It was the jolliest, happiest, most contagious laugh I've ever heard. You couldn't hear him laugh and not join in. He was a perfect gentleman, and I felt very comfortable being with him.

After the date, he dropped me off at my apartment and I just knew he would call me again the next day. But the day came and—silence. "Oh, he's probably busy," I thought. "After all, he is a firefighter. Certainly, he'll call me tomorrow." Silence. After a few days, I began to wonder why he wasn't calling. "Oh my goodness! He didn't like me." I remember feeling disappointed because, at that point, I really wanted to get to know him more.

I started to wonder what went wrong. Was it my outfit? Was I not his type? Or was it obvious that I didn't want him to try anything with me? That was probably it. When he had walked me out to his car that day, all my thoughts went south. The first thought was, "Oh brother, he drives a fine car, so he probably thinks he's all that." The next thought was, "Oh my goodness! I'm about to ride in the car with a man I don't know. What if he tries to make a pass at me?"

I didn't want to give him any indication that I was easy or interested in anything other than dinner, so after entering the car, I sat really close to the passenger door and kept my hand near the handle. I even had a plan if he tried anything: I was going to open the door and roll out of the car. Then after I was out, I would remove my shoes and start running and screaming.

(Sidenote: looking back on that date, I was so ridiculous. And after Cecil and I were married, he never stopped talking about that. Whenever anyone asked how we met, he always shared the story of how I "sat on" the passenger door of his car on our first date.)

But after the date, when I waited and waited for him to call, I worried that I had been a little too cautious. Finally, after about three or four days, the phone finally rang, and it was Cecil. We talked and laughed with each other for a while, and then he invited me for a second date to see a musical, which I accepted. I thought to myself, "Ooooohhhh, I got you now, brother! Watch this!" When he picked me up that night, I opened the door and he said, "Whoa!"

I giggled and thought to myself, "Mmmm hmmm . . . You thought you were dealing with an average one, didn't you? No, sir!" You see, I had to redeem myself after wearing that ready-for-war combat outfit on the first date. When he said we were going to a musical for the second date, I was too happy—that gave me an opportunity to pull out all the glam. I wore a full-length fitted dress, with jewelry, hair, and nails almost fit for the red carpet (not too over the top, though).

Throughout the entire night, he kept looking at me and smiling. I knew I had redeemed myself. It was another lovely date. This time when he dropped me off, he said, "I'll call you." I smiled and thought to myself, "We'll see."

The next day he called—and never stopped calling from that day on. In fact, I told one of my friends that I was becoming uncomfortable because he was calling so much. She told me to stop being silly and enjoy myself. I took her advice, and I'm glad I did, because one year after we met, he asked for my hand in marriage. After being engaged for a year, we were married on August 12, 1995. Nine months later, I gave birth to our first son, Brandon. Then twenty-one months after that, our second son, Jordon, was born.

We couldn't have been happier with our new family. I learned through Cecil what a loving father looks like, as my father wasn't present in my life that way. He was in and out of our home, leaving my mom to take care of my sisters and me by herself. Even when he was home, I don't remember him participating in our lives. He was just there.

Perhaps he started out as a more involved father, but when I was just a year old, my three-year-old brother was hit by a car and killed. When it happened, my mother was inside the grocery store. When she looked out the window, she saw my father jumping up and down in the street. He had witnessed my brother getting hit by the car. My mother said my father started taking drugs after my brother's death, and eventually he became a drug addict.

I don't remember much of my father, just him coming and going when I was little. But when I became a teenager, I started to see the abuse my father inflicted on my mother. The incidents were infrequent in the beginning. But as the years passed, he became worse. He would call her bad names, and they would fight. I would actually hear them hitting each other in the bedroom. It was horrible to feel so helpless. I wanted it to stop, but I had no control. So I would just sit and wait for it to be over. Then I would hear her crying, and I would cry too.

Eventually, he started hitting us girls too. I don't remember much, but I do remember that one day, while he was in a drug-induced state, he came into my room and socked me in the head. I hadn't done anything wrong. I was just lying there. I cried, and my mom was so angry.

Another time, my sisters and their friends built a clubhouse on the side of our house. But my mom made them tear it down because my father and his friends started shooting up in the clubhouse and they would leave dirty needles lying around.

In our later teen years, my sisters and I became angry and would try to protect our mother. I'll never forget the day that I decided to do something. I was on my way home from work and as I turned the corner, I saw my mother run out of the house, my father chasing close behind her. Oh my gosh! I sped up to the house, jammed the car into park, and took off running, my heart pounding with fear and anger. "Not this time! He's not gonna beat her. Not this time!" I ran as fast as I could, trying to get to her.

Our neighbor had told my mother that if she ever needed anything, she could come to her, so my mother ran next door to our neighbors' house. When I made it to the door, I could hear my mother screaming in their house as my father was trying to get in. The neighbor told my father not to come into her house. He tried it anyway, and she pushed him back out of her house. By this time, I had reached the door and I started pounding him as hard as I could, screaming, cursing, and crying. I didn't know what would happen and I didn't care. My knuckles hurt as I landed blows on his head. All of a sudden, he looked at me with an expression of total shock. Holding his head, he said, "Nunny!" That was my nickname. Then he stumbled away, and I don't remember anything afterwards. But that marked the day that I would no longer stand to see him hit my mother again. I didn't like him and wasn't afraid anymore. I wanted him out of our family.

Eventually, my father left us one last time. He moved back to Memphis where his family lives. Then one day the phone rang, and it was my aunt from Memphis. She was crying on the phone, and I knew what she was about to tell me. My father had died from a drug overdose. Although I didn't like him, I cried because I was sad that he had died. We went to Memphis for his funeral, but I don't remember anything about it. I had very bad feelings about him for a long time. It wasn't until I was an adult with my own children that I had to ask God to help me forgive my father. Then I had a talk with my mom, after which I realized how much resentment I'd held towards her for years because she stayed with him and allowed us to live in that environment. But after asking God for help, I was released from the bondage of unforgiveness. Forgiveness breeds life and freedom.

I was determined to never marry a man like my father. However, I allowed myself to get involved with men who were no good for me. I was never abused by a man, but I went through a bunch of frogs before my prince charming showed up.

Cecil was an amazing father. He did everything he could to be a strong presence in his sons' lives. When they were babies, he did just about everything I did. He changed the diapers and woke up in the middle of the night for feedings if he didn't have to work the next day. He crawled his big self on the floor with them. He taught them new words, dressed them, and put them to sleep.

When they were old enough, we enrolled them into sports and music lessons because Cecil wanted his boys to play ball and musical instruments. He never missed their games when he was off work. And he jammed with the boys on his bass guitar while they practiced their instruments.

He coached one of the Little League teams and assisted other coaches whenever he was available. He attended the boys' school events, cooked for their birthday parties, had the dreaded father-son talks, chaperoned at school camping trips, and helped teach when we homeschooled them for a short time.

Cecil taught his sons how to be men. He got in their faces when they lost their minds and acted as if they had no home training. And they respected him. He gave them a taste of entrepreneurship by starting a business for them to learn how to be business owners. He kicked their butts on the basketball and tennis courts.

He was no different with me. Oh my goodness! I was very well taken care of by my husband. We decided, before getting married, that I would be a stay-at-home mom after we started having children. Therefore, one month before our first son was born, I quit my job at the hair salon where I worked. Cecil made sure I was comfortable in our home, providing for my needs and supporting me in whatever I wanted to do. I joined a Mom's Club group to stay active and keep the boys connected with other children. I started two little side gigs once while the boys were little, as if being a stay-at-home mom wasn't enough.

I went to the local college, posted ads for typing services, and started typing papers for the students. Yes, they were still submitting paper copies of work back then. After I became bored with that, I signed up to become a consultant for the Pampered Chef and sold cookware and kitchen gadgets through in-home cooking parties. Cecil was happy to see me thriving in our community and doing things that made me feel good. He was especially thrilled about the Pampered Chef because I earned all the free products through my sales, which meant more kitchen gadgets for him to use in the kitchen. Once I earned all the cookware I wanted, I quit. Hahaha!

Cecil was an amazing cook. No, he was *beyond* amazing in the kitchen. The man could taste an item at almost any restaurant, then go home and recreate the dish. And most of the time, his rendition was much better than that of the restaurant chef's. He was so talented in the kitchen that we rarely went out to eat in our town because it was hard to find something that impressed us. We were food snobs. He prided himself with presentation. If the food wasn't pretty on the plate, he wasn't happy. But the greatest compliment you could give him was to say his food was delicious. He would light up like a Christmas tree whenever I raved about his food. And I loved to see him happy about his meals, so I made it a point to make sure he knew just how good it was. I always bragged on him to other people, and it made him feel appreciated.

Not only was he a great cook, but he was also very handy around the house. We very rarely had to call for repairs, because if he didn't already know how to fix something, he would find a video on YouTube and learn how to do it himself. Let me tell you, there's something so sexy about a man who can fix things around the house. There were many times when I just sat and watched my husband fix something and smiled, while thanking God in my head for the gift.

I never had to pump my own gas. Yep, that's right. The man kept my car gassed up. The only time I ran low was when he would be at work for two or three shifts in a row. I was so spoiled that I would not go to the gas station and put gas in my own car. I hated the smell and touching those pumps.

He used to get mad at me sometimes because he would get in my car and find the gauge on empty. I felt so bad, but I just didn't pay attention sometimes. If I took his truck when I needed to go somewhere, he knew exactly what was up. He would just go fill up my car and not say anything. When I would hug and thank him, he would either shake his head or laugh.

I was living the dream. I had a handsome husband who loved me like crazy. We had two beautiful sons. I was in the best physical shape that I had ever been in my life. I was thriving in my relationship with God and learning so much through reading my Bible. While my life wasn't perfect—like most families, we had lots of ups and downs—it also wasn't horrible. Sometimes I would think to myself, I can't believe I get to have this life. It was beautiful, happy, and lovely . . . until it happened: betrayal.

Chapter 2

Betrayal

When life seems to be going well, you don't expect trouble. And you don't always notice the little red flags warning that something is wrong. I was grateful for my life and thanked God often for my husband and children and felt extremely blessed with what I had. Then my peaceful little world came crashing down.

One day, after coming home from the gym, I received a phone call from my husband. We'd both been at the gym, and after I went home and he finished his workout, I knew he was headed to the grocery store. I assumed he was calling to ask me about dinner; after all, he'd already called on his way home from work to tell me what he was making. I was so excited—he was making one of his signature dishes. Oh gosh, I could almost taste it as he shared what was on the menu for that evening.

I answered the phone, but he didn't say anything. "Hello?" I said again. Still no answer. I heard voices in the background, so I thought maybe he was talking to someone while he was calling me. That's happened many times before—but this time there was no "Hold on, Nita," as he finished his conversation.

I heard a woman talking but I couldn't make out her words, so while I waited for Cecil to come to the phone, I got my towel and other items ready for the shower. I could tell the woman was complaining about someone, but I couldn't tell who. She went on and on, but I didn't hear my husband talking at all. So I said hello again, but no response.

Then I heard her say, "But yooooou . . ." I froze. It sounded like she was saying good things about my husband. Pressing the phone harder against my ear, I tried desperately to hear her words. Then I started to feel like something wasn't right. Who was this person?

I screamed into the phone, "HELLO!" Nothing. "CECIL!" Still nothing. Then the reality hit me. "Oh my gosh! He can't hear me. He's not answering. He doesn't know I'm on the phone. He must have pressed against the phone and dialed me by accident. He doesn't know I'm here, listening." My heart started pounding as I walked into the closet, not knowing what was happening.

The next words that came out of her mouth took me down. "I want to be with you so bad."

My heart *exploded*! As if in slow motion, I fell to my knees. "HELLO!" No response.

She kept talking. "We could go to the beach and then get into a jacuzzi." I couldn't believe what I was hearing. Was this woman asking my husband to sleep with her? Why wasn't he saying anything? Why wasn't he saying NO? Why was he there, with another woman?

He finally spoke and said, "Butt naked on the beach," and started laughing. My heart was pounding so hard that I could actually feel it in my neck. I grabbed my chest with my left hand, as if to keep my heart from falling out. Slowly, I leaned forward and allowed my head to rest on the floor, just above my knees, the phone still pressed to my ear. It hurt so badly. My heart was crushed. Putting my left hand to the floor, I pushed myself back onto my knees. My entire body was trembling. As I continued listening, trying to make sense of what I was hearing, I grasped the side of my head, with my mouth wide open. Shock! I put the phone on the floor and began rocking back and forth, staring at the phone, my arms wrapped around me. Breathing heavily, I felt tears begin to form in my eyes. I was afraid to hear more, afraid of what might happen. But I didn't want to miss anything.

I quickly picked up the phone again and heard her say, "What's for dinner tonight?" He proceeded to tell her what he was cooking for his family. "Awww, I want to be with you so bad, babe." I froze again. Babe?! She just called my husband *babe*?!

"HELLO!" No answer. If she called him babe, that meant they'd been seeing each other for a while. This was an *affair*! My husband was having an affair! "God, please help me! Please don't let this be happening. Oh, God!" I screamed *hello!* into the phone one last time, but he didn't hear me. The woman continued, "Remember that one time we went out?" He responded, saying, "You remember that?" WHAT!? Oh my gosh! He went out with her? My husband took another woman out? When? Where did they go? How could he do this? Rage filled my entire body. I wanted to know where they were so badly so I could roll up on the scene. She went on talking, then stopped mid-sentence. I heard shuffling, then silence. The phone went dead. He'd finally realized I was on the line. "Dirty son of a gun!"

I quickly called back, and he answered the phone. When he said hello, I heard the terror in his voice. "I can't BELIEVE you," I screamed. "You! YOU! I can't BELIEVE this! I hate . . . I hate . . . I HATE this! You dirty dog! You DOG! You did this?! Ohhh! I can't BELIEVE it!" I couldn't even talk, couldn't form a coherent thought. Rage, pain, disgust, confusion, shock—a wave of emotions swept over me. I wanted to tell him how much I hated him, but it wouldn't come out.

"NITA!" he called out, but I hung up the phone and stood up. The room was spinning as I stood there with both hands at my temples. I didn't know what to do. I looked around the closet at his clothes, thinking, "My marriage is over." I looked out the closet door toward the window where the sun was beaming through, and I thought to myself, "There's no more sunshine." I went down to my knees again, then rolled onto my back, placing both hands on my head with my eyes closed. It felt like someone was twisting my heart, tying it into knots so that oxygen couldn't reach it and it wouldn't beat anymore. I was so scared. What was I going to do? What about our sons? "Ohhh, God, my babies! This is gonna kill them. Our family is destroyed."

I knew he was on the way home, but I didn't want to see him. I hated what he had done to our family. I dreaded looking at his face. I didn't know what to do, so I stayed in the closet. My mind was spinning like crazy, so many questions swirling around my head. My initial shock hardened into intense anger, and I got up from the floor and started pacing in the closet. My fists began to open and close as my pace quickened. I wanted to start pulling his clothes down from the hangers, but I didn't.

I heard the garage door open and I stopped walking, listening for his footsteps. With each step I heard, my anger intensified. I wasn't ready for the confrontation. My mind said, "Hit him with something when he walks in. Throw things at him." But my heart said no. He entered the bedroom, came around the corner, and stood in front of the closet. Our eyes met. I had never looked at my husband with disgust until that moment. The man I had always viewed as strong and handsome became a pitiful piece of trash in my mind. As I looked at him, all I felt was anger. He opened his mouth immediately and said, "I'm here to own up to it. I did it. I'm not gonna lie. I messed up. But I never slept with her."

I held myself together—and the only one I can credit for that is God—and calmly asked, "Do you think that matters? The only reason I believe you is because I heard her begging. You've been seeing another woman behind my back. You had an affair. Whether you slept with her or not, it was an affair."

All of a sudden I heard, "WHAT?!" Our oldest son, Brandon, had walked in on the conversation. He was supposed to talk with Cecil when he got home, and when he saw his dad walking quickly through the house, he thought he was in trouble and followed. Brandon completely exploded on his dad and told him to get out of the house. My heart was broken. That wasn't how I wanted him to find out. I could see the devastation on Cecil's face. But it wasn't over yet. I didn't want our youngest son, Jordon, to hear about it either, but I knew we would have to tell him since the oldest knew.

When Jordon came home from school, Cecil went into his room and had a talk with him. Shortly afterwards, Jordon emerged, visibly upset, and headed out the door. I followed behind him. He took off walking and I caught up with him. There were tears streaming down his face. I grabbed him and held him tightly while he sobbed. "I can't believe this is happening," he cried. "I can't either," I replied. We started walking in silence. Before we went back to the house, I asked him to please allow me time to process this on my own without bringing other people into it. I couldn't handle anyone knowing about what happened. I was so embarrassed. I asked the same of our oldest son.

When I returned home, I told Cecil, "I can't stand your presence, so you need to leave this house." After a brief conversation, he packed up his work clothes for the next day and left. He sent me a text message to tell me where he was, providing the location of the hotel and room number. The next day, I didn't speak with him over the phone at all like we always did when he worked.

Over the following weeks and months there were tears, anger, conversations, and revelations. When I found out who the woman was, I became even more angry. It was a lady from the gym, someone who smiled in my face and spoke to me every day. We took Zumba class together. And she was married too.

When I went back to the gym the day after the discovery, before I knew who the other woman was, I remember how she looked at me. I walked in her direction to enter the class and she looked uncomfortable. I said hello, as usual. She said hello but was a little different. For a brief moment I thought to myself, "She acted differently. Could it be her?" Then I thought, "No, stop! Don't be paranoid and think every woman you see is the one." My intuition was spot on, though.

Cecil wasn't forthcoming with all the information at first, and that set me off. It wasn't a pretty scene. Eventually, he came clean, answering all my questions, and he told me who she was. I was shocked that it was someone I knew. But he lied about how long the affair had been going on. I searched the phone records and learned that they had been talking for two years. How could my husband be so cold? Who had he become?

I told him I wanted a divorce. We were in the office, and I was sitting in the chair. He dropped to his knees and begged, "Nita, please don't leave me," and tried to grab my hand. I quickly backed away from him, rolling across the room with a look of disgust on my face. His mouth fell open and the tears came. He got up and walked out of the room. A few minutes later, I walked into the room where he was sitting and asked him to refrain from seeing her until the divorce was official. He looked at me, crying, and said, "I don't want to see her." Still, I couldn't believe anything that came from his mouth because he had completely destroyed my trust in him. He asked me to please not put him in the category with all the other guys who had cheated. I said, "You put yourself in that category!" He shook his head in agreement. He already knew how I felt about infidelity.

I could barely wait to get to the gym the next morning. I stepped into the building, ready for a showdown. I had no intentions of working out that day. I went with one purpose only: to confront the woman who had an affair with my husband. When I spotted her, she was with two other women and it looked like she was helping them. I stood at a distance, not wanting to interrupt the other ladies. She saw me looking.

It didn't look like there would be a break where I could step in, so I walked over and said to her, "When you're done with them, I need to talk to you." She said okay and kept working with the ladies. I went over to the free weights, a few feet away, and began lifting just to occupy myself. When I saw her coming my way, I put the weights down. "What's up?" she asked, but I could hear in her voice that she knew exactly what I wanted to talk about. I wanted to slap her face for having an attitude, but I restrained myself and responded, "My husband told me the truth about you. I know he's been seeing you." Right away she started denying it and said, "We're just friends."

"Why would he tell me differently if you're just friends? And why didn't I know about the friendship?" I asked.

"I just talk to him about my problems, that's all."

"Yeah, he told me that your husband treats you like crap. So, what is your mode of communication with my husband?" I asked, trying to get her to admit that they had in-person communications.

She started walking away and said, "I'm not gonna sit here and answer all these questions." I completely stepped outside of myself and left all integrity behind. What happened next is totally not who I am. It's not typical of me to use bad language. I'm sharing it here because I want to tell the truth and allow you to see just how devastated I was at the time. I'm revealing my low point to show you that no person on this earth is above bad judgment, including Christians.

I followed closely behind her as she walked away, and I cussed that woman out and told her not to go near my husband again. She walked back over to the women she had been working with. I continued with my insults in front of them, calling her disgusting names. She said, "We're just friends. You better get out of my face." I responded, "Do you beg all of your male friends to sleep with you?"

What I wanted to do was grab her by the hair, throw her down, and stomp her face into the ground, but I didn't. I called her one last disgusting name and walked away. My blood was boiling, and I could feel my body trembling. I started to leave but changed my mind and jumped on a treadmill on the other side of the gym. There was a raging fire burning in my heart, and I needed to work off some steam. Also, I needed to apologize to the other two women before I left. Eventually I saw her leaving the gym, visibly disturbed.

Later, I saw the ladies exit the racquetball room right next to the treadmills, so I jumped off the treadmill and approached them. They both looked at me, and I said, "I just want to apologize first for interrupting your workout, and second for the disrespectful language I used. That is not who I am, but I just found out some devastating news about this lady and my husband." They told me it was okay and shared very encouraging words with me. Then one lady asked if they could pray for me. "Oh my GOSH! Yes!" I replied. God knew I needed those women at that moment. They grabbed my hand and prayed with their hearts, right there in the gym, as tears fell from my eyes. When they were done, we said our goodbyes. I hadn't seen them at the gym before, and never saw them again after that day. I believe God ensured those women would be there for me because He knew how foolish I would act on that day.

Before I continue with this story, I need you to know that I was wrong. I had no business going to the gym and cursing that woman out. I allowed my pain to bring out the worst in me. My husband is the one who stood before God and promised loyalty to me, not her. He was the one who looked into my eyes at the altar and said, "Forsaking all others," not her. Her actions were guided by her character and lack of respect for herself and the sanctity of marriage and had nothing to do with me personally. She wanted my husband and that's what she went after. I was wrong to try to handle the situation on my own, without seeking God's wisdom first.

The Holy Spirit wore me out about that. I felt horrible and had no peace. I apologized for calling her names the next time I saw her at the gym. But that didn't end well—I also told her I hoped she would find love again, with a single man, after her divorce. Yeah, I threw in a jab at the end, and that made her mad. I smiled, told her to have a nice day, and walked away.

Then I started searching online, looking up how to proceed with divorce filing. I was too embarrassed to ask anyone. I didn't want people to know that my husband had cheated on me. I still didn't understand how it could be our reality—he treated me so well. He never gave me the impression that something was wrong. But as time passed, I started remembering things and realized that there were a few signs that I missed because I didn't pay attention.

Cecil was on eggshells around the house. I didn't say anything to him for probably two weeks. I discontinued doing his laundry and everything else I had done to take care of him. But he never stopped taking care of me. He continued to cook the meals, put gas in my car, and everything else that was normal for him. The first time he cooked, I didn't want to eat his food. I hated his presence.

I didn't make it easy for him, and it was painful for both of us. We eventually started communicating again, and he asked me if he could talk to someone about this. I told him I didn't care what he did or who he talked to. Then he begged me to go talk to my girlfriends. He said I needed someone to talk to also.

I knew he was right, but I was too embarrassed. I had three friends I'd been close with for years, and we met once a month for lunch. I already had a luncheon planned for the girls at my home, but I cancelled and told them my marriage was over. I didn't give any further details. They were shocked. One of them reached out to me and said that they were there when I was ready to talk.

Eventually I reached out and said I needed to meet with them. They immediately set something up for that day. When I walked into my friend's house, all three of them were there waiting for me. We went into the family room and took a seat. I sat on the sofa, with one sister on my left, and the other two across from me.

"My marriage is over." Silence. They all had looks of deep concern on their faces. I started to breathe heavily, then slid from the sofa onto the floor and began to sob uncontrollably, bending over as if in physical pain. "I hate him!" Sobbing. "I hate him!" I looked at my girlfriend on the left and said, "I hate him," with a whimper. She shook her head as if to say, "It's okay." I continued crying and blurted out the words, "He CHEATED!" And I began sobbing even harder and louder. I heard my girlfriends crying with me and I felt their hands on me. Oh, my heart hurt so badly! I needed God's help!

After I calmed down, I told them everything. We talked and they spoke words of peace and encouragement into my heart. They allowed me to be in my feelings and never said a negative word about him. But one of them was very upset with him. As we continued talking for a while, trying to make sense of the whole thing, I felt blessed to have them in my life. They continued to be there for me, praying as God led them.

One day my girlfriends accompanied me to one of my son's tennis games at his school, where I told them I was filing for divorce. We talked for a while and one girlfriend, who had experienced a divorce many years earlier, advised me not to be so hasty to end my marriage. She warned me that a divorce would be exceedingly more painful than the affair.

But in my heart, I knew that I could never trust him again. At that moment I simply couldn't stand him. Being in his presence was very uncomfortable. Having watched another friend go through the process, I knew it would take a long time to finalize a divorce. I wondered what it would be like for us—we didn't have a history of fighting. But I was mad at him and didn't want to be nice. A divorce seemed like the only way forward.

Chapter 3

A New Beginning

O ver the next few months, Cecil and I began to work through what happened, and I decided to hold off on the divorce. I saw how hard he was working to keep our family together. After I decided to stay with him, we began the long road to recovery.

I had never seen my husband fight so hard for anything. He was determined to show me that he wanted to make it right. I told him how I felt about cheaters: once a cheater, always a cheater. He did everything within his power to try to prove me wrong.

One of the things we struggled with in our marriage was communicating when we got upset with each other. I always wanted to talk about it when there was a problem, but he would shut down to avoid an argument. While he thought he was doing the right thing and preserving the peace in our home, it was actually building resentment in me. We'd dealt with this for a while, but soon Cecil started talking to me more and engaging in the uncomfortable conversations. I was impressed but suspicious. Was he doing it just to get me back, or was he really changing on the inside? Whatever the case, as we continued to work through our mess, he kept talking.

My husband was very uncomfortable leaving the house without me unless he was going to work. He didn't want me to think he was out doing wrong, so he would text me when he made it to his destination and again to let me know when he was leaving. If it was taking longer than it should, he would call me to let me know why.

We were doing well—or so I thought. At one of the luncheons with my girlfriends, I shared with them how much better I was doing and that I was progressing with my healing. Well, shortly after that, I discovered that I was getting better at my husband's expense. While I was feeling comforted by all that he was doing, I stayed on his case and kept throwing certain parts of the affair in his face.

One afternoon, he walked into my sewing room with two glasses of wine and said he needed to speak with me. I smiled, thinking it was going to be something fabulous. When he started talking, I could tell something was wrong by the look on his face. He began to tell me how defeated he was feeling. He was trying to do everything to prove to me that he wanted our marriage to work but felt like he was still being punished for his mistake.

My heart sunk. I was speechless. We talked more and I started to understand why he was feeling that way. When the conversation ended, I knew I would have to do some deep heart work. If I really wanted to stay in the marriage, I would need to forgive this man. Up to that point, I thought I had already forgiven him. After all, he was still in the house and we were communicating. He had apologized over and over but I realized, in that moment, that although I told him that I forgave him with my words, I had not really forgiven him in my heart. I was holding on to my conviction of "once a cheater, always a cheater" and "a cheater is never to be trusted."

I never understood why women stayed in marriages when their husbands cheated. Granted, there were a few exceptions where I supported the rebuilding of marriages that had suffered betrayal. But for the most part, I just didn't get it. I hate to say this, but I thought women were stupid for staying.

My negative thoughts were relentless. "Have I become that stupid woman who stays with a man who cheats? What will people think? What would they say if they found out? They're gonna call me a fool. He's gonna do it again. If he cheated, it must mean he doesn't love me. But that's ridiculous. I know he loves me. But how can you love someone and do this? How can I recover?" I was afraid of becoming that woman—the one who stayed.

I had to make a hard decision right then. Either I was going to let the past go and move forward with my husband who was fighting so hard to heal and rebuild our marriage. Or I needed to file for divorce and leave. I remembered what my aunt had said once: "Don't ever let another woman come in and destroy what you have built." I decided to follow her advice.

Over the next few years, after that conversation in the sewing room with my husband, we fought for our marriage. It wasn't easy and I struggled terribly at times with my thoughts. On my part, it took a focused effort to leave the past behind us. But when I did, I saw the beauty of what was happening for us. Our marriage was blossoming. Communication was deeper than it had ever been. Disagreements were met with compromise, not just with me getting my way all the time. I was falling in love with my husband again—really deep love. I didn't even know our marriage had fallen into the dangerous zone of complacency. But because we did the intentional recovery work, we emerged better than we had been before. We were thriving and our family was safe again.

I couldn't explain as it was happening, but now I understand that our marriage was different because we weathered the storm together. We persevered through the pain, and as a result our marriage was stronger and our love deeper. Of course, I was the one who was hurt by the affair. However, my husband not only had to deal with the inner turmoil over what he did, but also had to face the pain of living with a woman who was disgusted with him. It wasn't good. But I can say, with full confidence, that our marriage became better than either of us could have ever imagined before the trial. I know, I know—it's hard to hear that, but it was our reality.

Now don't get me wrong. I'm not saying that other marriages will benefit from an affair. That's nonsense and I would never encourage anyone to be okay with betrayal. It's the worst. It's horrible. It's painful. And it's WRONG!

Yes, we had it rough for a while, but in the end, we survived one of the most devastating trials that a marriage can suffer (in my opinion). We looked at each other differently after that. We went on with our lives and continued to fall deeper in love with each other. My husband became very intentional about us. He had always been supportive of what I did, but he became even more involved after the trial. We learned how to nourish and protect our marriage with great intention, never allowing complacency to set in again.

Years later, we stepped into a sweet new season—retirement. Cecil had always looked forward to retiring early. His was determined to settle down before the age of 65, so he arranged things so that he could retire at age 57. He was healthy, strong, full of life, and ready for his big day. Retirement!

I drove him to his last twenty-four-hour shift at work on February 26, 2017. Our sons met us at the station, and we enjoyed all the festivities that took place on his last day of work. Traditionally, the retiree provides breakfast for the crew and any visitors who come by, so Cecil made his famous chicken and waffles for breakfast. Firefighters, captains, chiefs, and friends from all over L.A. stopped by to congratulate and say farewell to Captain Morris. The retirement announcement rang out over the intercom system to all the L.A. City Fire Stations. I had the honor of pinning his badge on him for the last time. The boys and I went on a call with him that day just to see him in action one last time. It was the end of an era; our sons had grown up in the fire station, and our oldest son, Brandon, even took his first steps in the fire station.

Cecil prepared his last big meal for the crew: ribeye steaks, mashed potatoes, broccoli, and a green salad. As the day wound down, the boys and I said our goodbyes and left him to finish out his last shift.

The next morning, February 27, I woke up bright and early with much anticipation about the day ahead. I got dressed and headed to the fire station to pick up my man so we could begin our new season of life. Rolling down the freeway, I jammed to his old school funk music and sang my heart out. "Flashlight! Aw, we want the funk! Never learned to swim, can't catch the rhythm of the stroke! Aqua boogie baby! Never learned to swim!" Oh, he loved his P-Funk music, and I was driving his car. The party was on, and I was ready to greet my fine, retired, and happy husband. I pulled into the parking area at the fire station, went inside, watched my husband chat with the guys, and then we headed to the car. As we pulled out of the driveway, all his fire brothers stood in front of the station, waving and smiling. It was such a beautiful sight. Cecil waved one last time, put the pedal to the metal, and we sped off.

I screamed, "We're outta here! Woohoooo!" He cranked up the music, I started dancing in my seat, and his signature laugh filled the atmosphere with an indescribable joy. We were two of the happiest people on earth at that moment.

We began our retired life journey with smiles and giggles every morning during that first week. Most firefighters host a big celebration after retirement. However, despite my efforts to convince him that he really deserved one after so many years of hard work, Cecil didn't want a party. I even convinced him to go as far as checking out a venue for the gala, but eventually he said, "This just isn't something I'm interested in doing." Disappointed, I backed down and respected his wishes to not have a party. After all, we did have his big retirement trip scheduled for that July, and the future was looking bright.

Little did we know, our lives were about to change forever.

Chapter 4

Tragedy Strikes

Around April, Cecil began experiencing discomfort at the back of his neck. He tried a new exercise at the gym with the kettlebell and thought maybe he had pulled a muscle. He discontinued that exercise and waited for the injury to heal while we continued working out daily. Instead of healing, he started feeling numbness in his left shoulder. He thought it was related to the neck injury, but then the numbness started traveling down his left arm, making it difficult for him to work out.

At this point, I suggested that he get checked out at the doctor's office. He refused and said he would be fine. Eventually, Cecil started to experience weakness in his left leg. I noticed a couple of times that when he was driving, his turns were very wide, and he also started losing his balance. I became very concerned and kept asking him to go see the doctor. Still, he refused.

By the end of June, his condition had worsened, and he had more difficulty with his balance. Finally, he agreed to see a doctor because the retirement trip was around the corner and we needed to know if he was okay. Our primary care provider referred us to a specialist who said Cecil had compression on the spine, wrote a prescription for medication, and said he was okay to take the trip and to come back for a check-up after returning.

The retirement trip was a Viking River Cruise along the Danube River in Europe, and it was one of his dreams come true. He had always wanted to travel to Europe. Unfortunately, while on the cruise, his condition declined even further. When we stepped off the bus to board the ship, Cecil fell to the ground and I screamed. I thought he had hit his head on the concrete, but that wasn't the case. The staff quickly rushed over to help him up. I could tell he was embarrassed, but I was worried. They gave him a cane to walk with at the hotel in Prague because his balance was really off. The medication wasn't helping.

Despite his condition, Cecil enjoyed himself as much as he could. He didn't allow the issues he was having to take away his joy. His laughter and jokes were the same as always. We weren't able to join our group of friends for any of the long walking tours, but we would meet them at the end to hang out. We enjoyed the riding tours, dinners, and other activities that took place on the boat.

By the grace of God, we made it home and set an appointment with another specialist. But before that date came, Cecil started falling more frequently and I was becoming increasingly more concerned about his health. On August 6, he had a terrible headache all day long and used over-the-counter painkillers for relief. The next day, on August 7, the headache was still lingering and eventually became more painful. That evening, as I looked into his eyes, I knew this wasn't just a regular headache. So I told him I was going to call 911—something was wrong. He said, "I'm not a medical emergency. Don't call. I just have a headache."

During his thirty years as a first responder, Cecil responded to a large number of medical calls that were non-emergencies and used valuable resources that could have been better utilized for more serious incidents. So calling 911 for a headache was a serious offense for Cecil.

I sat with him on the sofa where he had been sleeping since we returned from the cruise because he couldn't walk upstairs. I couldn't bring myself to turn in to bed that evening because I knew something was wrong. I asked him a question and when he turned his face in my direction, it was as if he was looking straight through me, like he couldn't see me. His eyes were glassy and looked tired. He wasn't responding to my questions properly. That was it! I grabbed the phone, ran upstairs to our sons, and told them I was calling 911 because something was wrong with their dad.

The paramedics showed up and started taking his vitals and asking him questions. I was shocked to see him perk up and fire off answers to their questions without missing a beat. I told them he wasn't responding to me that way. Then he said, "I know the drill. I know what they're gonna ask me. I have to be alert." They took him to the emergency room and that's when our lives changed forever.

After examining him, the ER doctor said that he needed emergency surgery for compression on the spine. Cecil and I talked it over quickly and agreed to get this over with so we could continue with our retired lives. But before they could take him into surgery, a neurosurgeon came over to his bed and said he wanted to take an MRI of his brain first.

After receiving the results from the MRI, the neurosurgeon motioned for me to come over to his computer. He proceeded to show me a picture of Cecil's skull with a large black area and told me it was a brain tumor. Silence. I gasped, stopped breathing, drew my hands to my mouth in shock, staring at the screen. Finally, I exhaled and said, "Oh my gosh!" I couldn't believe what I had just heard. My mind went blank and I just stood there for a few seconds, looking at the doctor then back at the screen. I didn't know what to do. How could my husband have a brain tumor? What did this mean?

My heart pounded as we walked back over to Cecil and gave him the news. He said, "Really? Oh boy!" Then the doctor put his face very close to Cecil's and said, in a soft voice, "I'm gonna take care of you." Later, Cecil told me that when the doctor said those words to him, he felt a sense of peace. The doctor scheduled surgery for the next day.

On August 8, my fifty-first birthday, my husband had his first brain surgery, where they removed some of the tumor for the purpose of conducting a biopsy. As I sat in the waiting room with our pastor, a couple of fire brothers, and one of my firewife sisters, I was hopeful it would not be what the doctor termed a "bad" tumor. While we waited, we chatted with each other and the conversation was normal, not sad or gloomy. I tried to remain optimistic, and having close friends there with me for support helped a great deal. Their presence was exactly what I needed for what would happen next.

The neurosurgeon walked back into the room after the surgery was complete and sat down next to me with a look that told me it wasn't good. Then he said the two words that exploded in my ears: "Brain cancer." I looked at him, in shock, and repeated, "It's cancer?" He nodded. Silence.

He continued, speaking words that I couldn't hear. When he walked out, I buried my face in my hands and broke down in tears. My first thought was, "Oh my gosh, my husband's gonna die!" As I cried, one of my fire brothers came over to me, put his hand on my shoulder, and said the words I'll never forget. He said, "Come on now. We say we believe in God, right? We're gonna fight this!"

When I heard those words, something rose up in me. As I felt a surge of energy go through my body, I began shaking my head and saying, "Okay," over and over. Head nodding. "Okay, okay." It was almost as if I needed to work up the energy within my spirit to respond to what was before me. The tears kept pouring and I heard my pastor's voice next to me, speaking words of encouragement.

I needed to see my husband. I couldn't bear the thought of him hearing this news. I had to be there for him. With that thought, my brain immediately shifted to survival mode. My husband was my only concern. At that moment, he was the only person in the world who needed my attention.

After they got him settled into the Intensive Care Unit, I was allowed to see him. The doctor met with us, shared the details about his condition, the prognosis, and plan for treatment. His next surgery was scheduled for four days later.

On August 12, our twenty-second wedding anniversary, Cecil had his second brain surgery, where they removed as much of the tumor as possible without causing more damage. When I walked into his ICU room afterwards, he looked at me, said, "Happy anniversary," laughed, and fell fast asleep. I stayed in the ICU with him, sleeping in the recliner next to his bed because I couldn't leave him alone. So many of his fire brothers kept showing up at the hospital that the staff had to start limiting the number of visitors to only a few at a time.

Over the course of his illness, Cecil endured countless ambulance rides to the emergency room. He underwent radiation therapy, chemotherapy, and other medical complications due to the cancer. He also suffered a deterioration in his mental status. And due to the loss of mobility on his left side, he became immobile and was rendered bedridden.

After his first radiation treatment, he began having seizures and had to be admitted to the hospital several times for treatment after that.

Usually after his seizures, he would come out of it just fine. But after being admitted to the hospital for a seizure on April 5, he didn't open his eyes anymore. I was very concerned that he wasn't opening his eyes, even though he could hear us talking to him. Also, he wasn't responding verbally anymore.

During the second day of this hospital stay, I was sitting next to Cecil with a fire brother when the doctor entered the room. After sharing what was going on with my husband, he said the words that cut my heart to pieces. "We're recommending hospice for Mr. Morris." Silence. He explained that if they moved forward with more treatment it would only be a matter of time before he was back at square one and the cycle would continue. I looked at my husband and remembered the conversations we had held over the years about what we would want should either of us become ill and faced with a quality of life less than desirable. I flashed back to the night before when I was talking to God and asking Him to help the doctors to be united in their decisions for treatment. I asked God to help me accept His will, no matter what it was. I knew that my husband would not want to continue suffering like this, so I told the doctor, "Okay."

I reached out my hand to shake his, grabbed it, and buckled over in tears. I reached out to the nurse standing beside me, and she began to cry with me. Letting go of her, I sat down in the recliner, crying. I felt the hand of our fire brother on my shoulder. I looked at my husband and couldn't wrap my brain around the reality that my husband was going to die. I couldn't imagine how life would be without him. I hurt for him more than for myself, though. I recalled how excited he was to retire, all his plans to cook his favorite meals, to travel and enjoy his retired life. We were looking forward to growing old together, becoming grandparents one day, getting on each other's nerves, and just being together all the time.

When everyone left the room, I stood up from the chair, walked closer to my husband, and asked if he heard what the doctor said. He still hadn't opened his eyes, but he nodded his head yes and began to cry. Oh, my heart exploded! My knees felt weak and I really don't know how I managed to remain standing. I held his hand and rubbed his arm. The doctor came in and asked if I needed referrals for care facilities. I told him I would be taking care of my own husband at home.

Later that day, my husband's fire brothers showed up and escorted him home for the last time in the ambulance from the fire station that he had retired from. Although the hospital wasn't in their jurisdiction, the department approved the escort. I walked behind them as they pushed him on the gurney out of the hospital to the waiting ambulance. I witnessed the amazing pride and love of these brothers. Every step was taken with intention as they escorted him to the rescue. This was their brother, and they wouldn't have it any other way.

I had determined that when my husband came home to live out his final days, he would know how much he was loved. I allowed anyone who wanted to come visit with him; although he couldn't open his eyes or speak, he could still hear us. I have no idea how many people walked through the doors of our home, but one thing's for sure: my husband heard the voices and words of love. He felt the gentle caresses and kisses from our family, friends, and fire brothers.

Prior to the announcement that Cecil was being placed into hospice care, our church had planned a prayer vigil at our home. The vigil was supposed to be a time of prayer for healing, for a miracle from God. After I told them he was starting hospice care, we all decided to move forward with the prayer vigil anyway. From April 13 to the 14, people walked our block, praying, for twenty-four hours. They sat on the grass in front of our home, reading Bibles, praying in groups, and prayer walking around our home. One of the families parked their RV outside the house so that people could go inside to pray if needed.

While I didn't see everything because I was busy tending to my husband, the bits and pieces I did witness were the most beautiful moments. My husband's transition had begun, and I felt as if we were ushering him into the hands of God during that prayer vigil.

Three days later, on April 17, 2018, at 10:00 a.m., with me, our sons, and our pastor by his side, Cecil took his last breath. Silence. Tears. Emptiness. Grief. My husband was gone. The amazing man I met on the boardwalk at Venice Beach twenty-four years earlier had left me. My heart has never felt the agonizing pain that I experienced in that moment. I didn't know what to do or say. I wanted to be there for our sons, and that's all I could think of at the time. My heart hurt for them, and I wanted them to be okay.

The following weeks and months were all a blur for me. And though I had intense pain in my heart, I also had an indescribable peace. There was a strong presence in the midst of the pain. That presence was God. He began to reveal Himself to me in a way I had never experienced. I thought my future would be simply picking up the shattered pieces of my life, allowing God to heal my heart, and surviving. Soon I discovered that God had much more in store than just surviving. A shift was about to happen that would lead me on a journey I never had imagined. A journey of discovery. A journey full of tall mountains to climb. A journey of obedience.

I didn't understand at the time, but later it would all begin to make sense. Later, I would notice an awakening to how God was using the trials of my life to help me STEP into His purpose.

Many people discover, early in life, what their purpose is and how they intend to bring value to both their own lives and the lives of others. They follow their hearts, take risks, and focus on the important matters that lead to intentional living. They're not paralyzed by their fears, nor do they make decisions based on what others may think of them. They consciously walk in the truth of who they are, welcoming challenges and obstacles as opportunities for growth. I've always admired these people.

Then there are those who go through life, fitting in where the world says they are best suited. They know deep within that there's more they have to offer, but the fear of failing, or even succeeding, keeps them from exploring. They're the ones who allow their gifts and talents to be exposed—but only to a certain degree. To avoid shining too brightly, they downplay the power that lies within. They want everybody to like them, so they walk the safe route of being what they think others want them to be.

Then one day, tragedy strikes. For some who have been reluctant to show up in all the fullness of who they are, it's the storm that awakens the power to STEP into God's purpose. The reality that life will never be the same again ushers them into an awareness of who they really are and what they need to do in order to show up healthy and whole on the other side of the tragedy. Through the trial, they begin to lay down the burdens that formerly held them captive. Through the storm, they realize they need to be liberated in order to walk in the truth, fullness, and obedience to God's purpose. If that's you, keep reading and embrace the power of stepping into what God has for you.

Chapter 5

An Important Message

The message I'm about to share with you sits at the core of my being. It's the foundation upon which my life is built. It is because of this message that I am able to stand in my faith, trust the sovereignty of God, endure the trial with grace and proceed to God's purpose—all while living in the midst of the storm.

Unless you have a basic understanding of what the gospel message is all about, some things I say in this book will be foreign to you. For that reason, I want to present the full gospel here in the simplest way that I can, just in case you've never heard it.

Even if you already know the good news about our Savior, a reminder is always refreshing. You can never hear the gospel message too many times. In fact, I believe that it should be engraved on our hearts, planted in our memories, and spoken often.

Romans 10:12–15 in the NIV version of the Holy Bible reads:

"The same Lord is Lord of all and richly blesses all who call on him, for, 'Everyone who calls on the name of the Lord will be saved.' How, then, can they call on the one they have not believed in? And how can they believe in the one of whom they have not heard? And how can they hear without someone preaching to them? And how can anyone preach unless they are sent? As it is written: 'How beautiful are the feet of those who bring good news!'"

So, please, allow me to be the beautiful feet in your presence as I share the good news of Jesus Christ.

The Gospel Message

The Bible teaches that "if you declare with your mouth, 'Jesus is Lord,' and believe in your heart that God raised Him from the dead, you will be saved" (Romans 10:9).

Saved from *what* though? This is where it begins.

God created the world and everything in it. He created the world by speaking it into existence. When He created the first man, Adam, He created him in His own image from the dust of the ground. Then He created the first woman, Eve, from a rib he had taken from the man. God saw all that He created as good. God is not a created being. He has always existed and is eternal. He lives forever. Therefore, since He made humans in His image, that means we were created to live forever also (see Genesis 1–2).

He gave Adam and Eve a place to live, the Garden of Eden. They had everything they needed within the Garden to live the perfect lives God had created for them. He permitted them access to everything in the garden, with the exception of one tree. He told them they were not allowed to eat from the Tree of the Knowledge of Good and Evil or they would die (see Genesis 2:15–17).

Well, God had an adversary, someone who used to be the highest of all His angels. He was given the name Lucifer, which means "star of the morning." He was the model of perfection, beautiful and wise, and had great influence. Lucifer wasn't satisfied being a servant of God. Instead, he wanted to be God, so he got kicked out of heaven. This fallen angel is now referred to as Satan, the devil, or the enemy. Since then, there has been a spiritual war between God and Satan, good and evil. Satan's main objective is to deceive people and keep them away from God (see Ezekiel 28:12–17 and Isaiah 14:12–15).

One day Satan presented himself to Eve in the Garden, disguised as a serpent. He began to ask her questions regarding the tree she and Adam were instructed not to eat from. After she shared God's command, Satan told her that God didn't want them to eat from the tree because, if they did, they would have knowledge like Him and know good and evil. Eve was deceived into eating from the tree and encouraged Adam to do the same (see Genesis 3:1–6).

This was the first sin. Sin is disobeying God. As a result of their disobedience, God placed a curse on Adam and Eve. And because of this curse, every person after them would be born into the world with sin. Therefore, we're all born with a nature to disobey God (see Genesis 3:16–19).

God hates sin. His penalty for sin is death. Since we're born into sin, we're all doomed to death. This is called the wrath of God. But God had a plan of redemption from the beginning. In order for us to be saved from eternal death, someone had to die in our place (see Romans 6:23).

God has a Son, named Jesus. He chose His only Son to be the sacrifice for our sins. He sent Jesus down from Heaven, into the world, to die in our place so that we may be saved from His wrath. Jesus obeyed God, took our sins upon Himself, and died a brutal death by crucifixion on a cross (see 1 Peter 2:24).

But that's not the end of the story. After Jesus was buried, He rose from the dead three days later. He overcame death. After His resurrection, He ascended back into Heaven to take His seat at the right hand of God. At the appointed time, which none of us knows, Jesus is coming back. He's coming back to gather all the people who believe in Him, and He's taking us to live with Him in Heaven forever (see 1 Corinthians 15:4, Acts 1:9–10, and John 14:3).

The Bible tells us that Heaven is a place of perfection, where there is no sickness, pain, death, or anything bad. We will be perfect in Heaven. This is eternal life for those who believe in Jesus Christ (see Revelation 21:4).

Remember, I said we were all created to live forever. Therefore, I believe that even those who don't believe in God will have eternal life. However, their eternity will be in a place called Hell. The Bible describes Hell as a place where there will be weeping and gnashing of teeth and eternal separation from God (see Luke 13:28).

In order to be saved from the wrath of God, you must believe in His Son, Jesus Christ. You repent of your sins by confessing them to God and turning away from them. After you have believed, God sends you a Counselor, called the Holy Spirit. He comes to reside inside of you, serves as your Guide, and helps you to live for Jesus. This is the gospel of Jesus Christ (see Romans 10:9 and John 14:26).

If you're hearing this good news for the first time and have decided to believe in Jesus, welcome to the family! Also, I have three pieces of practical advice to share with you:

1. Please don't try to navigate this new journey alone. You need people to walk alongside you. Find other Christians to help you learn and grow in your faith.
2. If anyone tells you that life is a piece of cake as a believer, it's not true. Don't believe it. In Part 2 of this book, I share very practical steps to building faith and identifying your identity in Christ. It will help to guide you in your new faith.
3. Learn the gospel by reading it often. Know the gospel by planting it in your heart. Share the gospel with others in your life so that they can also have an opportunity to believe in Jesus Christ.

Personally, I have no recollection of when I first believed in Jesus. My journey into faith began as a little girl (I'll share more about that in the next chapter), but there was no specific moment of transformation that I remember. Some people have beautiful stories and memories of when it happened, where they were and how they felt the moment they believed. I love to hear about incredible transformations, where God speaks to a person in the middle of the most unbelievable circumstance and at that moment they believe in Jesus Christ. Then there are those who have near-death experiences that cause them to believe. Whenever I hear great stories of transformation, I sometimes wish I had an incredible story to tell. But I don't.

All I can say is that Jesus is real, and He wants you to believe that He exists. If I had not been changed through my faith in Jesus, I wouldn't be sharing what you will learn in this book. The evidence of His existence, for me personally, is manifested by the internal changes that have taken root in my heart. Because someone decided to share the Good News about Jesus Christ with me one day, my life was changed, and this is my testimony.

Part 2

STAND

"Therefore, everyone who hears these words
of mine and puts them into practice is like a
wise man who built his house on the rock.
The rain came down, the streams rose,
and the wind blew and beat against
that house; yet it did not fall, because
it had its foundation on the rock."

(Matthew 7:24–25)

Chapter 6

Seeds of Faith

Have you ever been faced with something so difficult that all you could do was stand? I'm not talking about a physical stance; I'm referring to a mindset. There are some moments in life that literally take your breath away—when you actually find yourself focusing on your inhaling and exhaling to make sure you are still breathing. You know that you're alive but have no idea what to think, say, or do. You don't know how your heart keeps beating because your pain feels deadly, like you could die at any moment from heartbreak.

My husband's death was that moment for me.

After receiving the shocking news about his health, I knew I would need a lot of help to walk the journey that was ahead of us. One word kept coming to my mind throughout his illness and even more so after his death: STAND! At first, I thought it meant I needed to be strong. But that wasn't it. It soon became clear that I needed to allow my faith to uphold me. I needed to STAND in my faith.

But what would that look like? Was my faith deep enough to carry me through the aftermath of his death? I had no doubt that it would. You see, I had already experienced the power of God's presence during my husband's illness. And I knew that the same power that kept me in those times would remain with me in the coming days, months, and years. You may wonder how I could be so confident about the painful journey ahead—but I wasn't confident in the journey. My confidence was in Jesus. I didn't always have that depth of faith; it grew and matured through the years. When I look back over my life, I see just how God was preparing and grooming me for the trial.

Planting the Seeds

When I was a little girl, my mother used to send my sisters and me to church while she stayed at home or worked. There was a bus that picked up all the neighborhood kids and drove us to church every Sunday. I don't remember much about those visits to church, only the bus rides. We had so much fun on the bus. When we were a bit older, probably upper elementary- and middle school-age, we would walk to church, sometimes fighting on the way. One day a large group of us girls were walking to church and another group, who had been waiting along the way, came out to fight us. Well, they chose the wrong group that day, because we beat the girls down and continued on to church.

In our household my mom was on her own most of the time, caring for three daughters, because my father was in and out of the house doing his own thing and not providing for the family. My mother had to work—sometimes multiple jobs at once—to take care of our needs. I don't recall going to church with my mother much as a young girl, but I do remember hearing her pray every morning in the bathroom next to my bedroom. Every morning, without fail, I lay in the bed and heard her whispers from the time she entered that bathroom to get ready for work until the time she exited.

We were expected to go to church, however, when my mom would send me and my sisters to Memphis to visit with our grandmother (MaDear). We always looked forward to those visits because we got to see all our cousins, hang out with our friends on MaDear's block, and eat all the amazing Southern food. I remember how we would argue over who would sleep in the tall, four-poster bed with her every night. The one thing we didn't like about our time with MaDear was visiting one family member's house in the country. It didn't have a bathroom indoors, so we had to go to the outhouse to relieve ourselves. I will never forget the horror of having to trample through waist-high weeds to enter that little box and look into the hole called the toilet. Oh gosh, just the thought of it brings back horrible memories. I was so afraid that a snake or some other critter would come while I used the bathroom. I was a city girl, and this made my entire body tremble. After I was done, I would run as fast as I could back to the house.

Every Sunday during our visit, MaDear would also take us to church in the country. I remember how she would get all dressed up, but I don't remember much else—other than her telling us to be quiet in church.

Then, when I became a young adult, I began to attend church on my own. I went to church just to hear the pastor make me feel good with his preaching. That was it. I didn't read the Bible on my own or participate in any church activities. I was fascinated with how he could take one scripture and talk for over an hour. But sometimes I wished he would just be done because I was hungry and wanted to go eat.

The churches I attended were very charismatic, with large choirs, dancing in the aisles, jumping up and down (we called it shouting), and yelling out during sermons to express agreement with the pastor. I have to admit, there were times when I went to church anticipating what the people in the congregation were going to do. How would they dance today? Who was going to fall out shouting, and how many people would it take to pick her up from the floor? How long would it take before the pastor was panting and running across the pulpit while preaching the Word of God?

When we attended church back in the day, everybody dressed up. You would never catch a woman in church wearing jeans. Some churches didn't allow women to wear pants at all. The older women had their "seats," and you'd better not sit your body down in the spots they had claimed for themselves. We called them the Mothers of the Church, and the Mothers would tell you the truth about yourself if you got out of line. If your skirt was too short, one of the Mothers would let you know. If you showed up baring shoulders or any skin was exposed that the Mother deemed inappropriate, she would certainly give you a look.

Even though I attended church as a young adult, I never felt like I really belonged, like I was one of them. I had my life, and it didn't include living for God. While I believed in Jesus, I just didn't know much about Him other than what I heard the preachers share. And once I left church, well, I never really put much thought into doing anything about what I had heard. I mean, in my mind, I wasn't a bad person. I was hardworking, I paid taxes, and I tried to be nice to people.

Each time I went to a new church, I would stand up to be saved when there was an altar call—I didn't know any better. The altar call was an invitation to believe in Jesus Christ. I thought that because I had not been attending church and was out in the world living in sin and switching churches, I needed to repent and be saved again and again. Nobody had taught me any wiser because I never made myself available to learn about the faith. I never wanted to be like the church people; I thought they might be boring. I thought they would want me to be this perfect, holy person who couldn't have any fun if I joined their circle.

Because I had no knowledge about the faith, I just didn't want to get too close to them. In my mind, they thought they were better than I was. However, there were some who made me wonder. I remember seeing them shouting in the sanctuary, then I'd later see them out in the parking lot cussing or gossiping. I had a strong side eye, and I certainly didn't want to be around them. In fact, I was more turned off by them than I was by those who I deemed perfect.

Not long after I met my husband, in the early nineties, I started attending a new church in Los Angeles and became very intrigued by the messages. There was something a little different about this church than all the others I had attended before. I found out they had a New Members Class where you could learn about the church to decide if you wanted to join. I had never heard of that before.

I signed up to attend the New Members Class and was very excited to learn more about the church. On the first day of class I was surprised as I walked in and saw a room full of people. As I took my seat, the instructor began to share about the church, the different ministries, and living as a Christian. She had me captivated, and I kept attending the classes to learn more.

By the time the course ended, I had already become engaged to be married. I remember talking to the instructor one day about marriage counseling because she suggested that I consider it before getting married. I purchased the workbook but after telling my fiancé, it became apparent to me that he wasn't interested. Oh no!

You see, he wasn't attending church when I met him. He had grown up in the church with his family but stopped going at some point. When I explained to him how I was really enjoying this church and wanted to join, he said something that caught me off guard. He said, "I just don't want things to change." My immediate response was, "Oh, nothing's gonna change." I had no idea what I was saying at the time. I had no idea about the seeds that had been planted in me already that would bring about exactly what my future husband didn't want: CHANGE.

I never went back to the instructor about marriage counseling because she wanted to meet him and he wasn't interested. I told him that we needed to have marriage counseling and we could do it on our own with the materials that I purchased from the church.

So, we went through the workbook and completed the course on our own. Then we were married and started having children right away. After Brandon was born, I knew that I was going to need help raising a child. I needed God, but I didn't really know Him. I was ready to apply myself and I needed someone to teach me how to KNOW God.

Chapter 7

The Search for Home

As I settled into my new role as mom, I began searching for a church home in our new town. I visited so many churches, trying to find one that came close to what I had experienced in my old town. I was shocked to find that none of the churches had choirs, only worship teams. With each visit I became more disappointed because I wasn't finding what I had experienced in L.A. Then it hit me—"You're not gonna find that here. Pray and ask God where He wants you to be."

I prayed, asking God to please help me find a church. Then one day, I decided to try another church that I had found in the phonebook, Desert Winds Community Church. At the time, they were holding Sunday Services at one of the local high schools. I got Brandon dressed and headed to the church. Cecil was always at work when I tried a new church. His only request for a church home was that they offered an early service. This church had an 8:30 a.m. service, so that was perfect. When I walked to the entrance, the pastor greeted me and introduced himself.

He informed me there was nursery care for my son, but I was very protective and didn't want to leave him with strangers. So I took him into the service with me. I enjoyed the service, but I think I left early because my baby wasn't quiet. I was torn about going back because I didn't want to leave him in the nursery, but I also didn't want him to disturb the service. I decided to go back and was shocked when I approached the door and the pastor addressed me by name. I'm pretty sure I gave him a stunned look. "How in the world was he able to remember my name?" I wondered. "With all the visitors that walk through these doors, is he actually remembering each name?" I was very impressed and felt even more welcomed after that.

I took a seat and once again enjoyed the service. Besides the warm hospitality I received from the church members, I was also drawn to the manner of preaching I observed. It was different from what I had grown up with. The pastor was more reserved, and I wasn't sure if he would be able to make me feel good like the other pastors—remember, I went to church to feel good. The congregation was different as well. They were quiet, no shouting or dancing. "Why are they so quiet?" I wondered. "Why isn't anyone agreeing with the pastor while he's preaching?" At some point during the service, Brandon became fussy, and if I recall correctly, I left early again. This time I didn't go back for a very long time.

It wasn't until my son was two or three years old that I decided to go back to the church. By this time, I had given birth to Jordon, and the church had moved into another building. I began attending more often and started meeting people. Then they announced that Vacation Bible School was coming up and all children ages two and up were welcome. I thought to myself, "I would never leave my baby with strangers and leave the building. No way!"

Nevertheless, on day one of VBS, I walked through the doors of the church with Brandon and handed him to the lady and her daughter who were overseeing the toddler class. He started crying and I stood there. How could I walk away from him like that, leaving him with a bunch of strangers? What kind of mother would do that? What if they're not nice to him? What if another kid hits him?

The lady who took him into her arms told me that he would be okay. She reassured me, "They cry the first time, but when the parents leave they're just fine." I thought to myself, "Yeah, you probably say that to all the parents. You're just trying to get me to hurry and leave." Of course she said that to all the parents—it was the truth, and she really needed me to get out of there.

I started walking away and as I looked back, my baby was crying and reaching for me. "Dear God," I thought, as I paused. She said, "It's okay. He'll be okay." I turned and walked through the doors with my heart melting. After the doors closed behind me, I looked through the window and he was still crying. "Oh God, I can't take this!" Then I took a seat outside the door for a few minutes because I was just messed up about leaving. When I heard the music begin to play, I stood to peek in again. She was still holding Brandon, but he wasn't crying. I waited a little while longer and peeked in again, and sure enough, he wasn't crying.

At that moment I started for the exit, walked out into the parking lot, and entered my car. I sat there for a moment, pondering if I should leave or just go sit outside the door until it was over. Taking a deep breath, I put the key in the ignition, started the car, looked over at the front door of the church, and backed out of the parking spot. That first day, I couldn't think about anything else. As soon as it was over, I hurried to pick up Brandon, jumping out of the car and speed walking toward that door, my heart pounding, wondering if he was okay.

When I finally laid eyes on him, he was just fine. The teacher told me he played with the other children and had a fun time. Every day that week I took Brandon back, and as he became more comfortable with being separated from me, I became more comfortable with attending the church. I needed to feel safe with the people in the church who would care for my child while I attended service before I could become a regular.

I kept attending and getting to know people. One day, after service, a church member invited me to join the hospitality team as a greeter. I was surprised; I didn't know I could have a job at the church as a new person. After she explained what the job entailed, I accepted the invitation. This was the very first time I had been an active participant in a church. This was the beginning of my journey into learning about my faith.

What I would soon learn was that knowing about Jesus is totally different from KNOWING Jesus. Knowing about Him has to do with what you learn about Him, what you hear about Him, what you read about Him. On the other hand, *knowing* Jesus is about experiencing Him. As one experiences Jesus, a transformation takes place. Going to church every Sunday isn't enough. Attending Bible studies every week isn't enough. So how do you come to *know* and experience Jesus?

Any kind of learning requires more than just reading for knowledge's sake. To be transformed by learning, you have to immerse yourself in what you're learning. I didn't realize it at the time, but accepting the invitation to greet people at the church on Sunday mornings was my first step into learning how to serve God. This may sound so simple, but you don't know what you don't know until you learn it for the first time.

Soon after I began to serve through greeting, they announced that the New Members Class was starting. Oh, I was beyond excited. This was an opportunity for me to learn more about the church and possibly become a member. Cecil had already attended and was fine with the location, so he was on board with us joining this congregation.

I showed up to the class with so much excitement—I love being in community and learning with others. The pastor went over all the things we needed to know about the church to help us decide if we wanted to join. I joined right away. For the first time, I felt like I had a church home, a place where I could learn and grow. I wanted to learn as much as I could and really KNOW who Jesus is. Soon I would learn what it meant to experience God.

Chapter 8

Learning to Experience God

One Sunday, during church announcements, I heard that there would be a class called "Experiencing God." The title alone was enough to pique my interest. I *had* to be in this class. I signed up and showed up the first evening with a smile on my face and a pep in my step. There were about seven or eight of us in the class, and when it was over, I knew I would never be the same again. It was in this class that I learned what it means to have a personal relationship with Jesus. I don't recall ever hearing that phrase before—or if I had, it went right over my head.

One of our assignments was to learn how to listen to the voice of God and the different ways He speaks to us. I was completely in awe and wanted more information. I was surprised to learn that He actually speaks to me in more ways than just reading the Bible, like through other people, circumstances, prayer, and dreams. Then I started thinking back to times when I may have heard the voice of God but wasn't aware. It was all so very fascinating.

During one class session, we were discussing growing in our Bible knowledge, and the topic was Bible Studies. I shared with the group that I didn't attend any Bible Studies at the church because there weren't any offered during the day. Evenings were not an option for me because I had my children. Then one of the guys in class spoke up and said, "Start one of your own." I think my heart stopped for a few seconds. I thought to myself, "What in the world is this man talking about? I don't know the Bible. Doesn't he know that I'm new to this stuff?" I shared with him that I had no knowledge of the Bible to be trying to lead anybody. The instructor told me that I didn't need to know everything. He said I could facilitate a Bible Study and learn with those who attended. I started feeling butterflies on the inside because, as he was speaking, I was agreeing with him in my spirit. But my mind was telling me I was some kind of fool to think that I could be in charge of a Bible Study. All the class members started encouraging me to just give it a try. I walked away that evening wondering what was happening and I thought back to the lesson on hearing the voice of God. I remember praying that night for God to let me know if this was His voice.

On the first day of Bible Study, I walked into that Sunday School classroom at the church with fear and trembling. People had signed up to join the study and showed up on the first day. A couple of teenagers watched over the little ones in the nursery. I don't remember what that first study topic was, but I do remember how nervous I was about being in a leadership position. While I was told that I was simply facilitating the meetings and didn't have to know everything, I still felt some sense of responsibility for those who were coming to study with me.

I facilitated the Bible Study for a few years, moving the study from the church to my home, then back to the church again. I learned a lot over those years about how to study the Bible. I also attended another class the church offered, called Bethel Bible, where I was able to learn even more about God's Word.

I began to volunteer for Vacation Bible School every summer as a teacher. Because it was only for a week, I felt it wasn't as scary. I enjoyed spending time with the children and seeing the excitement in their eyes. Then one year, after VBS had ended, the Children's Ministry Coordinator came walking towards me, and I knew instinctively what she was coming for. She spoke the words that made my heart begin to pound: "Anita, you do an amazing job teaching at VBS. Would you consider becoming a Sunday School Teacher?" Oh my gosh! My thoughts went wild. "Why, God? Why is she asking me this? Doesn't she know that I don't know everything? Doesn't she know that I need to learn more before I can teach these kids? What if I tell them the wrong thing? Am I a teacher?" But even with all these questions, I already knew what the answer was. I said yes.

Never would I have imagined that teaching children in a Sunday School class would be some of the most informative years of my faith journey. Because I didn't want to steer the babies in the wrong direction, I knew I had to take my preparations for these lessons seriously. These children were little sponges and very impressionable. I needed to have my stuff together if I was to lead God's most precious ones. If I steered them wrong, I would be in trouble.

I took great care in preparing for the Sunday School lessons, incorporating activities and events to complement whatever we were learning. I wanted to make sure that I used different learning styles. In the process, I was learning more about the Bible, faith, Jesus Christ, serving God, and living for Him. I was growing in my faith as I served God's children.

I decided that I needed to teach the children the books of the Bible in order. But how was I going to do that in a way that would capture their attention and help them to remember? The more important question was, how would I teach them what I didn't know myself? The answer to that question came quickly. We would learn together.

I started making lesson plans and creating lists and activities for us to learn these books. Then I came across a children's song that taught the books of the Bible. I had never heard the song and didn't even know such a thing existed. With this song, the kids and I learned the sixty-six books of the Bible together. There I was, a grown woman, a mother of two, learning the books of the Bible from a children's song.

I taught Sunday School for seven years and was allowed to follow the group that I began with in preschool all the way through fifth grade, at which time I handed them over to the Youth Group.

During my days of teaching Sunday School, I also joined the Women's Ministry Team at church and served on the board for a time. I was able to observe other women of faith and grow with them as we served other women in the church. As that final year of teaching Sunday School drew closer to the end, I began to feel overwhelmed, like something was missing. I began to desire a deeper connection with my God. But more importantly, I felt like I wasn't as present in my own home as I was at the church. I was doing so much ministry outside of my home, that I began to feel like I was neglecting my family.

Transformation

One day I heard something in my spirit that shocked me. The instruction was to simply "Go home." I didn't get it. What did this mean? For days I pondered it and prayed for clarity, then it finally hit me. I needed to focus on my family, which was my first ministry. I informed the Children's Ministry Director that I would be stepping down as Sunday School Teacher after my group of children transitioned to Youth Group. At the same time, I withdrew from my position on the Women's Ministry Board. By this time, I had already turned over leadership of the Bible Study to another woman in the church. After I received the call to step down from everything, I told her I would no longer be attending the study.

I couldn't believe what was happening. It didn't make sense to me. In my mind, serving God meant doing all these things. How could I serve God and not be part of a Bible Study? How could I serve God and not be part of any church ministries? How could I serve God and not do what I saw everyone else doing? These questions plagued me as I submitted to what I believed I heard. What I didn't know was that this was the beginning of a transformation in my thinking.

While I was taking time away from outside ministries, I continued to attend church services. Then one day I began a personal Bible Study of my own on the book of Romans in my home, with just Jesus and the Bible.

I gathered my Bible, a notepad, and a journal and found an online sermon series by John Piper called "The Greatest Letter Ever Written."[1] It was a study on the book of Romans, and it was so intense that there were several days in which I had to stop because I couldn't see through my tears as I took notes. This was by far the most powerful study I had ever experienced.

I woke up each morning with anticipation for what I would learn and how my heart would be overwhelmed with awe. I had never been

---

1. John Piper, "The Greatest Letter Ever Written," Desiring God, www.desiringgod.org.

so moved by a Bible Study before. With each lesson, I took notes, created bullet points, wrote summaries, drew diagrams, and studied what I was learning. Each day, I started the study by reviewing my notes from the previous day to make sure I understood what I had learned. Then I would move forward.

One day, as I was studying and going through my notes, I remember being overwhelmed by a feeling of gratitude. I felt a heaviness upon me that I still can't describe. It was as if the presence of God was right there, in the room with me, teaching me, showing me His truth, feeding me, preparing me. He was preparing me. I remember stopping, at one point, and sitting back in my chair. I'll never forget this as long as I live. Holding my right hand to my chest, I spoke aloud, "God, I don't know what you're preparing me for, but I know you're getting me ready for something. Thank you, God. Thank you for whatever you're preparing me for." I left the desk and throughout that entire day I couldn't stop thinking about how powerful the presence of God was in that room. I couldn't shake the feeling that He was preparing me for something in the future. While I didn't know what it was, in the back of my mind, I knew it would be a difficult situation—a life trial. Looking back, now I realize that this was the building of a foundation, a planting in preparation for the storms.

Chapter 9

Life Preparedness Kit

Your ability to STAND in the midst of life's trials is directly associated with the depth of the spiritual roots planted inside of your heart. Whether you have been planting those roots for years or are new to the faith and only just beginning, what you have planted in your heart will reveal itself in the face of devastation.

The desire of God's heart is for you to be deeply rooted in Him. For this to take place, you must make yourself available to the process. I have some practical suggestions to help you learn how to plant, nourish, and grow spiritual roots over time. These are the steps I've taken over the years in applying myself to faith. In the beginning, I didn't realize that my efforts were building a foundation that would serve both me and others in times of hardship. But that's exactly what happened, and it can happen for you too.

You need to be prepared before the storm hits in order to STAND in the midst and in the aftermath. However, preparing yourself in advance takes time. It doesn't happen overnight. But when you invest the necessary time, you will reap the benefits when you have something to help you through the storm.

Allow me to use the event of an earthquake to illustrate my point. In the state of California, we have earthquakes, and they come without warning. When it happens, we move into action, using whatever safety measures we've learned to protect ourselves and stay safe.

Many years ago, I learned that the safest place to be during an earthquake was underneath a doorframe. I don't know where I learned that, but I believed it and always followed the directive until early July 2019, when we had several earthquakes in a matter of days. The first day, I sat at my sewing table doing what I love, when all of a sudden, I felt a familiar wave of movement. As usual, I paused to see if it would continue. Then it began to shake a little, so I stood up and started walking toward the doorframe. But before I made it to the door, the movement stopped. Back to the sewing machine I went to resume my sewing. The next day, another quake hit, but this time with more shaking. I quickly rushed to the door and stood under the frame, waiting for the shaking to subside.

After this series of earthquakes, I was listening to a news reporter, who said that the doorframe theory originated with an old image of a collapsed adobe home where the only thing left standing after the earthquake was a door frame. Therefore, people had concluded that standing in the doorway was the safest place to be during an earthquake.

In reality, he said, underneath a doorframe was not the safest place. This theory didn't take into account the fact that not all homes are adobe homes, or the possibility of flying objects hitting you, or not being able to brace yourself during intense shaking. It also didn't take into account the fact that doors are attached to most doorframes. During intense shaking, the doors would probably swing back and forth, which could cause bodily harm. Needless to say, I will no longer stand underneath doorframes during an earthquake. Being equipped with more knowledge helped me to make better choices about my safety.

As a measure of preparedness, many Californians have earthquake kits. These kits hold essential items in the event of a shortage of life-sustaining supplies, should stores and homes become inaccessible. Some families keep their kits in place and updated just in case the BIG one happens. Others don't really pay it much attention until there's an earthquake. The problem with waiting until an earthquake happens to prepare is that the supplies you need may be inaccessible or scarce.

In the same way, when you prepare ahead of time for the personal storms of life, you find yourself tapping into your internal source—that which is planted inside of you. You find yourself recalling what you have learned to help you push through the difficulties that accompany your trials. The same way that Californians have earthquake preparedness kits to help them in their times of trial, you can also get prepared ahead of time for any personal life storm that may come your way. Remember, God never promised you a problem-free life. So let's get you set up in advance. And just in case you're already living in the midst of a storm, this will help you too.

Allow me to introduce you to what I call the Life Preparedness Kit (LPK). The LPK will be the foundation upon which you STAND in the midst of any life trial. Before you can stand in confidence, you must first believe that you're standing on a solid foundation. You need to know that it's firm and strong enough to hold you.

Have you ever walked down the street or through a parking lot and come upon one of those metal grates with open holes or a manhole cover? What do you do? Do you step on it, step over it, or go around it? I do *not* walk on those covers—I don't want to be the one person who falls through. I know that may sound entirely ridiculous, but I have no confidence in those metal coverings. In my mind, there's potential for malfunction. But when I'm walking on concrete, I don't have a care in the world because I have full confidence that the concrete will not cave in and take me down. Whether I'm walking, running, or crawling, I believe the concrete will hold me up. Like concrete, the LPK will help you build confidence to STAND in the midst of your trials. Let's take a look at the elements of the kit.

Chapter 10

Faith

Faith is the foundation of the LPK. Without faith in God, the other items simply don't make sense, nor will they be of any interest to you. I like to think of faith as the tote bag that carries all other items in the kit. It does not matter how much faith you have at this moment; all you need to get started is a tiny seed of faith.

I know it can be a struggle, especially if you're new to the faith, when you see other people who appear to have it so together, spiritually speaking. They fire off Bible verses without even stumbling. They know all the stories in the Bible. Their prayers are elaborate, filled with fancy Christian words. They know the books of the Bible from Genesis to Revelation. They know just the right scriptures to use when encouraging others in their times of need.

Sometimes you can find yourself wishing you had all that knowledge. I know—I've been there. However, don't allow yourself to get caught up in looking at "people" and comparing yourself against them. This is one of the enemy's weapons against you. If he can get you to believe you don't measure up or that you don't have what it takes to be of any service to God, his job is done. However, when you fix your eyes upon God, allowing Him to be the Author and Perfecter of your faith, everything else falls into place as it should. Then the question becomes, "How can I exercise the faith I've been given to bring glory to God?"

The amount of faith God gives to another person is appropriate for the journey He has designed for them. Your position in His kingdom serves Him based on how He has designed you. God is the only One who knows what's ahead for you. He has apportioned faith to accommodate your life. It is your responsibility to recognize and exercise it. Start from where you are and watch Him strengthen your faith over time.

Saving Faith and Living Faith

There are two different types of faith, and you need both. First, there is saving faith—the faith that secures your future with God. This faith says, "I believe in Jesus Christ." If you skipped Chapter Five, where I go into detail about the Gospel of Jesus Christ, I encourage you to stop here and go read it now.

Then there is living or acting faith. It's the faith you exercise in your daily living. It's how you conduct yourself based on what you believe about God. It's what you project into the world in relation to what you know about His character as revealed in the scriptures. It's applying your spiritual beliefs to the everyday issues of life.

There are two stories in the Bible that demonstrate living faith from opposite angles. The first story is found in Matthew 14:22–31 and gives the account of Peter walking on water. When Peter saw Jesus walking on the water, coming toward him, he called out to Jesus. "'Lord, if it's you . . . tell me to come to you on the water.'" Jesus told Peter to walk on the water. Peter got out of the boat and began to walk on the water. But when he looked down at the waves, he became afraid, began to sink, and called out to Jesus for help. In His true nature, Jesus saved Peter from drowning.

So, what happened? Peter didn't exercise his faith to the fullest by continuing to walk on the water. He became distracted by the waves and began to doubt, even though Jesus was right there with him. Jesus had given Peter enough faith to come to Him on the water, but Peter wasn't fully trusting in God to uphold him in the waves, so he began to sink.

Jesus's response to him was, "You of little faith." This is the same God who said that if you have faith the size of a mustard seed, you can move mountains, or you can tell the mulberry tree to go into the sea, and it will obey you. He wasn't speaking literally here. What He was saying is that a small amount of faith that He apportions can accomplish great feats. He had given Peter enough faith to come to Him on the water, but Peter didn't believe.

Then there's another story in Matthew 15:21–28, when a Canaanite woman went to Jesus for help because she wanted Jesus to heal her demon-possessed daughter. Jesus ignored her requests at first and His disciples told Him to send her away. Then Jesus told her He was there to help His people, but she continued asking. He told her that it wasn't right to give to her what belonged to His children. She responded by saying she would take the leftovers, the crumbs. This woman believed that God could do what she asked, so she approached Him with expectancy and persisted. She never gave up. She didn't allow the disciples' displeasure to move her. She didn't even allow Jesus's responses to turn her away. Because she was confident in His character, she pursued Him relentlessly. She exercised her faith to the fullest and Jesus's response to her was, "Woman, you have great faith!"

Now here's something to keep in mind. Jesus helped both people. He saved Peter from drowning, even though he wasn't exercising his faith to full potential. And He saved the woman's daughter as she put her faith to work fully. Neither of them had control over what Jesus did based on their faith. God will NOT be controlled by your faith or anything else. Exercising faith is an act of obedience that promotes spiritual growth.

Some believe that asking for what you want "in faith" is a guarantee that you'll get it. They claim that when you don't get your prayers answered the way you wanted, then you didn't have enough faith. I don't agree with this line of teaching.

When my husband was sick, I believed with all my heart that he would be healed. Nobody on this earth can convince me that Cecil died because I didn't have enough faith. My husband is not here because that was part of God's plan. He knew Cecil was going to die on April 17, 2018. He allowed it to happen, and that's just the way it is. I don't understand it and I don't need to. I choose to believe in the Sovereignty of God, which we will talk about in the next chapter. For now, just know that having faith in God allows you to STAND in the midst of your trials.

Chapter 11

Purpose

Once the faith foundation has been established, the next item you will need to secure in the LPK is purpose. Some of the most often asked questions among people of faith are, "Why am I here? Why do I exist? What is my purpose?" These are valid questions to ask yourself because purpose should be the driving force directing the decisions we make in life. A lack of purpose yields a lack of direction, which results in a lack of destiny. If you don't know where you're going, you will always end up nowhere.

About a year into the grief process, I started to examine my life. When I found myself doing something I really didn't want to do, I would question, "Why am I doing this?" If I found myself in a place where I wasn't thrilled to be, I'd ask, "Why am I here?" I started paying attention to the decisions I was making and kept asking myself, "Why?" Finally, I came to the realization that I continued to do a lot of things because they were familiar. There was no good reason other than they had become habits—habits that no longer served me in my new season. That's when I vowed to myself that I would no longer engage in activities and spend time doing things just because I always had. I decided it was time to become more intentional about my choices. After all, my life had changed in a big way.

While we're having this conversation about purpose, I want to make sure that your focus is aligned properly. When you ask, "What is my purpose?" what exactly are you focusing on? The focus is on YOU. You're thinking about what you can do or accomplish. As human beings, our natural tendency is to focus on ourselves first.

However, when you're seeking to live a faith-filled, God-centered life, your main focus should always be on God. Instead of asking "What is my purpose?" your question should be, "What is God's purpose for His kingdom?" When you take the focus from self and place it on God, your perspective changes. Then the question becomes "How can I align myself with God's purpose?" It changes from "What am I gonna do?" to "What is God going to do through me to advance His kingdom"?

Of course, at this point you may still be wondering, "But I still don't know what my purpose is." Let's break purpose down into three parts.

1: Overall Purpose

As a believer of Jesus Christ, your overall purpose in life is to glorify God. Period! To glorify God means to bring attention to Him, to elevate Him, to please Him. Everything you are—the thoughts you think, the words you speak, your daily behaviors—should seek to glorify God. It's why you exist. To glorify Him in this way, you must allow Him to have complete liberty in your life, to work in and through you. As you walk in obedience to the calling He has placed on your life, He does His work to reach others.

2: Calling

Your calling is God's assignment for you in a particular season of life. Being called to serve God in one way now doesn't mean it will remain the same for the rest of your life. Some assignments are lifelong, while others are seasonal.

When my children were little, God called me to teach Sunday School at our church. Later He called me to homeschool my sons for a short time. After my Sunday School kids graduated to Youth Group, He called me to start a girls' club, where I mentored and taught them how to be young ladies of Christ. After the girls graduated from high school, the club ended as they went off to college and work. Then came a new season.

I was no longer teaching children. However, God allowed me to launch a sewing blog where I teach the basics of garment construction and encourage women as I boldly live out my faith.

After my husband's death, I was introduced to yet another new season. God has called me to speak publicly and write this book to encourage and teach others how the trials of life can lead to His Purpose. My next season will be determined by God.

As you can see, in my case, God has called me to different areas of service, but all with a similar theme: teaching. This leads to the next point.

3: Gifts and Talents

Your gifts are your instruments of worship to God. God gave me the gift of teaching, and as you've heard, He has called me to exercise this gift in the different areas and seasons of my life.

Your talents are the skills God has given you to be used in your calling. Sewing is a talent, and He allows me to use it to reach women all over the world, bringing attention to Him as I live out and share my faith. When you step into the purpose, calling, and gifts from God, others will be drawn to Him. The three must work together for there to be an impact on the lives of those God has placed in your life.

Let's combine the three to understand how they work together: Your purpose is to glorify God as you step into your calling—the assignment He has for you in a particular season of life—using the spiritual gifts and individual talents He has given you to bless other people.

Now, I don't want you to miss this most crucial part about living in God's purpose and calling. It's not about you. That's the simple truth about purpose. A lot of people get purpose wrong because they're only focused on how they will benefit. But when you're focused on God's purpose for His kingdom, you'll realize that it's much greater than you. It's about serving other people. Even in the suffering and grief of your circumstances, it's possible to serve others by staying in step with God, allowing Him to use your situation to glorify Him.

You have a desire that God has placed into your heart from birth. You were designed with purpose as a major ingredient in your spiritual DNA. You may not have always known, on a conscious level, what that desire or purpose is. However, there has always been a subconscious awareness within your soul. As you become more engaged with who God is and strengthen your faith, that desire begins to stir within you. And sometimes when you experience a life trial, you gain a heightened awareness, and your desire begins to grow.

I have a slogan, a saying that I share at the end of my sewing blog posts and YouTube videos. It reminds me of what I need to do in order for God to be glorified through me. This is my personal mantra.

"When you live in your DESIGN, it is from there that God SHINES!"

When you live according to the way you have been created, you position yourself to be used by God to bless other people. When you step into the assignment God has called you to, using the gifts and talents He's blessed you with, being totally authentic to how He has designed you, others will be drawn to Him. And that's how He is glorified.

Chapter 12

Bible

When you decide to build a spiritual foundation for your life, you're going to need some guidance along the way. We have been given a precious gift, a treasured resource that has all the teachings and wisdom we need to learn how to build and live on that foundation. This resource is the Holy Bible, the spoken Word of God in written form. The scriptures were spoken to men of God's choice and recorded in the Bible for all generations to live by.

You cannot become deeply rooted in Christ without reading the Bible. Even if you go to church every day of the week, if you neglect reading and learning His word for yourself, you miss out on a crucial element in the life of a believer. I realize that there are many reasons people choose not to read the Bible. And I wonder if you've ever had any of these thoughts.

"Oh, gosh! I don't understand everything in the Bible."

"I get confused about what's going on and it takes me a long time to find verses and different books."

"The Bible seems boring to me, and I find myself falling asleep."

"I would rather just follow along at church and have them tell me what it says."

Trust me, I get it. I've been there. I still don't understand everything in the Bible. In the early days, when I didn't know the books of the Bible in order, it took me a long time to find the verses in church. And by the time I found a verse, the pastor had already moved on and I would totally miss whatever he had shared. Everyone still used printed Bibles back then. Now, everything is digital, so all you have to do is type in the verse on your smartphone or tablet to have it in front of you within seconds.

Instead of using the table of contents, I would keep my head straight down into the book, peeking over at the person next to me to see which direction they were turning. I didn't want them to see that I didn't know where the book of Joshua was or that the book of Acts came right after the Gospels. I would peek at the table of contents occasionally but tried to be inconspicuous about it. I chuckle now when I think about that because— *why?* Nobody cares if you use the table of contents. And nobody cares if you don't know the books in order.

Of course, as time passed and I used the Bible more often, I became more familiar with the location of the books. But as I shared earlier, it was a children's song that helped me learn those books.

Although you may encounter obstacles as you begin to read the Bible for yourself, the many benefits far outweigh the struggles. One of the greatest benefits is an assurance that you have firsthand knowledge directly from the Word of God. This is important as you listen to the teachings of others, whether they be pastors, Bible Study leaders, or anyone who teaches from the scriptures. When you have a familiarity with the scriptures, then you'll be able to recognize when and if you're being given wrong information.

There was a group of people in the Bible, the Bereans, who checked Paul's teachings against the scriptures. Paul was a highly respected and trusted source of the teachings of Jesus Christ in his day, but the Bereans weren't willing to simply take Paul's words as being true until they checked for the validity of what he was teaching.

If you're a new believer, I recommend joining a Bible Study group or connecting with someone mature in the faith to help you learn how to study the Bible on your own. God has the power to open your understanding and give you knowledge and wisdom, but you must do the work.

When you begin to read God's Word, it helps to have a strategy to become consistent with the practice. The key to being successful is to create a system that works for your personality and lifestyle. Here are some tips that have helped me, and I hope they will encourage and inspire you to develop consistency in your Bible reading.

Set Aside a Time of Day

Like every other important part of your day, Bible reading should have its own scheduled block of time. When that happens is up to you, but I suggest scheduling it for your most productive time of day. The ideal time would be when you are most alert so that you're able to give the best of yourself to God. However, I realize that many factors—like family and work—will play into this. Perhaps there are other activities you can either eliminate or spend less time with to make room for this important part of your life. If you have small children, consider scheduling your time for when they are sleeping, at school, or in bed for the evening. The goal is to schedule a time where there are no distractions.

Choose a Space

Make yourself comfortable in a place where you can have quiet, uninterrupted time with God. That may be a chair in a quiet room in your home, or in your car during lunch break at work. Perhaps you want to go elaborate and decorate a spare room in your home as a designated prayer room. Even if you need to go outdoors to your patio for a quiet escape, just create a place.

My place is a recliner in my bedroom by a window. I keep a fluffy throw on the chair during cooler months to stay warm while reading. Sometimes I have fresh flowers and a scented candle on the nightstand next to the chair. To set a calming mood, I often have my phone playing peaceful piano instrumentals at just the right volume. On days when I set the mood in this way, I have the best Bible reading times.

Create a Reading Kit

I can't tell you how many times I've sat down to read my Bible and realized I didn't have something I needed. I get up, go to another room to retrieve that item, return to my chair, and sit back down only to realize I've forgotten something else. Then one day I had a lightbulb moment. I thought to myself, "I need to have everything in one place." Immediately, I went through the house, gathered all the items I used during my daily study, and created a Bible Reading Kit. Game CHANGER! Oh my goodness! Now, when I go into my quiet space to read, everything I need is always there. No more up and down, searching for missing items.

Creating a Bible Reading Kit will help you to be more prepared when you sit down to read. If you want to create a kit of your own, I've listed below all the items that I use in mine. Add items that help you enjoy your reading time.

Of course, you will need a Bible—and there are many different versions on the market. When I was younger, I had no idea. I thought there was only the King James Version because that's all I had ever heard or seen. Some believe that other translations are watered down and don't capture the fullness of His Word. I will disagree and leave it there. Choose a few verses or passages and read them from different versions of the Bible to see which you understand best, and go with that version.

Daily Devotional

The market for devotionals is vast, so you can find books on various topics to use for daily inspiration. When my husband died, a dear friend gave me a devotional about grief that was very helpful as I navigated the early days of his passing. Choose a devotional that meets your personal needs.

A word of caution: don't allow the devotional to take the place of your Bible. Devotionals should be used as a supplement only. I usually read mine after reading the Bible message for the day. In the past, I used it first to prepare me for the main reading of my Bible. Develop a method that works for you, but keep the Bible elevated higher than the devotional.

Journal

If you like to write your thoughts and prayers, having a journal in your kit is helpful for the times when your spirit wants to release onto paper the words building up in your heart. This doesn't have to be a forced activity. Just allow it to flow naturally. I find that when my heart is heavy or I'm experiencing an overpowering sense of fulfillment in His presence, I want to write. Use the journal to your advantage without putting pressure on yourself.

Notepad

Have you ever been reading your Bible and found your mind wandering off to thoughts that had nothing to do with what you were reading? That's what your notepad is for. When the random thoughts enter your mind, stop reading, write down the thought, then return to where you went off track in your Bible. Of course, you may choose to use your smartphone instead. Either way, it really works to just get those distractions out of your head. Then, after you complete your reading, you can take the list of thoughts and do whatever you choose.

Index Cards

A huge part of becoming deeply rooted in Christ is planting God's Word in your heart by memorizing scripture. I create scripture cards and use them every day to learn verses and passages that I want to commit to memory. This valuable practice provides strength, peace, and wisdom that I can call upon at any time, no matter where I am. Speaking God's Word in a moment of joy or when you're filled with grief is the most powerful act of worship.

To create your own cards, follow these steps:

1. Whenever you come across a Bible verse or passage of scripture that you want to memorize, pull out an index card and write the verse. Don't forget to record the name of the book, chapter, and verse on the card for reference.
2. Hole punch the card in one corner and place it on a metal ring.

3. Read your scripture cards every day until you have memorized the verses.

4. After memorizing a verse, either keep it on the ring as a reminder or remove it. I have an index card file box where I keep all memorized cards.

I tend to focus on verses relating to areas where I struggle. For example, if I'm struggling with negative thinking, the verses on my ring will all center on the mind. I learn scriptures that will help me to focus on transforming my thoughts to honor God.

Another great tip for storing your cards: create several rings with different themes. Perhaps you need to memorize verses about faith. Create a ring of verses about that topic. Then, maybe later you find yourself struggling with forgiveness. Create another ring of verses to strengthen you in that area. Get creative! Try color coding the cards, giving each theme a designated color. If you have a Cricut machine, you can go all out and make your cards extra special. For those of you who are card makers, the sky's the limit on how you can use your talent to decorate your scripture cards.

If you love this idea of having scripture cards but have zero desire to make them on your own, I've got you covered. I've created a file that you can use to print scripture cards for negative thinking onto cardstock. All you have to do is cut them apart, add hole punches, and insert a metal ring.

Go to www.anitabydesign.com/scripture-cards for more information about the scripture cards.

Pen/Highlighters

Of course, you will need a pen if you plan to journal or do any other writing during your reading time. Highlighters can be used to outline things that really speak to your heart, things you want to see again when you return to that page in the Bible. I use different colors to break up thoughts, ideas, themes, etc. If you don't like marking your Bible, you can use color-coded sticky note flags.

Bookmarks

Most Bibles come with attached ribbons to be used as bookmarks. However, sometimes you may want to save more than one page. If you're reading from the Old and New Testaments at the same time, having multiple bookmarks is very helpful. I use them in my Bible and devotionals and usually have five or six bookmarks in place at a time.

Readers

If you wear reading glasses, I highly suggest having a separate pair for your Bible Reading Kit. If you don't, I guarantee you there will come a day when you sit down and get all cozy and comfy before realizing your readers are in another room. Just keep a separate pair in the kit. You will be glad you did—I promise.

Basket

You will need a place to keep all your items together. I have a basket for all my items, and I keep it on the nightstand next to the chair in my bedroom. It has a handle, which makes it easy to carry should I decide to read in another room. If you don't have a basket, use anything that will hold all your items. Try using a tote bag, storage bin, or decorative cardboard box.

Bible Reading Plan

Next, you're going to need a reading plan. This is for focusing solely on reading through the Bible, not studying. There are numerous Bible study methods. To learn more about how to study the Bible, I suggest reaching out to a leader in your church or someone mature in their faith to guide you in that area. Or you can Google it.

I suggest making a commitment to read through the entire Bible every year. There are many different annual reading plans and Bibles that can assist you with reading through the Bible in a year. I've listed a few options below:

- **Bible in a Year:** These are Bibles arranged by date so that you don't have to figure out how many pages to read each day in order to finish within a year. All the work is done for you—no calculating pages and dates.
- **Chronological Bibles:** The Chronological Bible records the books, chapters, and verses in the order that the events are believed to have taken place. If you prefer to read the Bible this way, choose a one-year chronological Bible. Again, no planning on your part because all the work is done for you. Just follow the reading plan in the book.
- **Online Reading Plans:** There are hundreds, maybe even thousands, of Bible reading plans online that will guide you through reading the Bible in one year. Type "Bible in a year reading plan" in your preferred search engine and you'll discover a multitude of options.
- **Gordon's Bible Reading Plan (my favorite):** I use a plan that was designed by my Bible Doctrine teacher. Using his system, you complete the Bible in one year by reading three chapters from the Old Testament and one chapter from the New Testament every day. He organizes the plan by months and chapters. I've been most successful in my daily reading with this plan. For a free copy of this reading plan, go to https://www.anitabydesign.com/bible-reading-plan.

Prayer

Finally, you'll need what I consider the most crucial item in the kit: prayer. Why is it the most important part? Because the enemy doesn't want you to study, and he'll distract you in every way. In contrast, God definitely desires you to spend time with Him by reading the Bible, so He will bless your time together with Him.

Always begin your reading time with prayer. Pray as you are led by the Spirit of God. My prayer before reading consists of the following:

1. I start with praise to God and thanksgiving for His presence.

2. I seek forgiveness for my sins, through confession, so that I may be in right standing with Him.
3. I ask for clarity that I may have understanding as I read.
4. I pray for protection over my mind so that I may focus.

That's it! I highly recommend coming up with a strategy to help you read the Bible. When you make it a part of your daily life—as instinctive and important as eating, sleeping, and breathing—you will see the power it yields in every area of your life.

Chapter 13

Prayer

I've talked about the importance of praying before reading the Bible, but prayer, as a part of life, is also an essential element of the LPK. It's your way to communicate with God. That's what prayer is, a conversation with God. However, in order for it to be pleasing to Him and beneficial for you, it must be a two-way conversation.

Have you ever been engaged in a conversation with someone who did all the talking and you kept waiting for a chance to jump in, but they never paused? I've been in that situation so many times and it isn't pleasant. Unfortunately, there have been times when I zoned out and stopped listening because I felt the speaker had no interest in a two-way conversation. At that point, I'm looking for a way out. I want to end the one-way conversation.

I've often wondered how God feels when we go into prayer and talk the whole time, leaving no room for Him to speak. I can't help but think that He, too, may be waiting for a pause from us in our prayer time so that He may speak His wisdom into our hearts. As I mentioned earlier, I learned to hear the voice of God while taking a class at my church. When I first decided to practice listening during prayer, I wasn't sure—it felt strange to sit in silence for any length of time. But when I began to experience the amazing voice of God through the promptings of my spirit, I knew that I needed to continue.

I Don't Know How to Pray

I've heard people say, "I don't know how to pray." I believe everyone knows how to pray. We all know how to have a conversation with another person, and we've already established that prayer is simply talking to God. When I hear someone say they don't know how to pray, I think they're drawing conclusions from what they've seen and heard from others. They hear another person pray and think to themselves, "I don't know how to pray 'like that.'" That's why it's important to keep in mind that prayer is personal to you. It doesn't have to look or sound like anyone else's prayer. Your posture doesn't have to mimic what you've witnessed from others. Your words don't have to be churchy and verbose for Him to hear you. Present yourself to God as you are. He wants authenticity. The *real* you! He already knows everything about you, including your thoughts. He doesn't want a carbon copy of someone else.

Some people have routines that they follow as they approach Him in prayer; others don't. Some kneel; others sit or stand. Some pray with closed eyes; others talk to him with eyes wide open. Many pray in their regular language, while others pray in spiritual tongues. Some have to be still, and others pray on the move. Some speak with elaborate, spiritual words, while others converse with God like they're talking with a friend (which they really are). In order to get comfortable with prayer in your life, just make yourself available to Him and be yourself.

If you're new to praying, there is a passage in the Bible where God actually tells us how to pray. It's called the Lord's Prayer, and you will find it in Matthew 6:9–13. Jesus gave this as a guideline to tells us what we should pray about. Many people recite this passage as their prayer and others use all the elements of the passage to guide their personal prayer time. You will become more comfortable with prayer the more you do it.

Asking

While prayer isn't *just* about asking for what we want, if we're being totally honest with ourselves, asking constitutes a large portion of our prayer time. For that reason, I want to spend some time addressing how the Bible teaches us to approach God with our petitions.

This may seem counterintuitive, but a big part of asking God for things we need and want is listening. In our effort to have our needs met, we often overtalk and don't spend enough time listening. You've probably heard it said that God gave us one mouth and two ears for a reason—so that we will talk less and listen more.

When submitting your requests to God, take time to pause and listen for His voice. This practice requires patience, and in the beginning it feels awkward. Because we are so fast paced in our living, silence has become uncomfortable. There's so much noise and so many voices clamoring for our attention that it's sometimes hard to discern the voice of God among all the rest. However, the Bible says that God's sheep hear His voice, He knows them, and they follow Him (John 10:27). We, who believe, are His sheep, and to hear His voice, we must be listening. So how do you listen while praying?

This will be personal to you, but I'll share with you how I listen. I ask God for something that's on my heart. After submitting the request, I stop talking and sit in silence for a while. Sometimes I hear an answer in my spirit and sometimes I don't. After I've listened for a while, I go back to praying.

There have been times when I have sat in stunned silence after receiving what I will call a divine download—an answer to my prayer in the time of silence. I've also been blown away by the times God has allowed me to speak the answer from my own lips while praying. This is something that requires intentional listening, but the rewards are bountiful. Give it a try the next time you have prayer time. If you're like me, you'll be excited when you hear the answer to your prayer.

Guidelines for Asking

We are given a set of guidelines from the Word of God that we should follow in our time of prayer when it comes to asking Him for the desires of our hearts. Let's take a look at what some of those scriptures teach us.

Ask

In Matthew 7:7–8, the Bible tells us to ask, seek, and knock. When we do these three things we will receive what we've asked for, find what we were seeking, and the door upon which we've knocked will be opened.

... In His Will

We learn in 1 John 5:14 that we can be confident that He hears our prayers if we are asking for that which is in His will for our lives. But how are you supposed to know His will? This is where reading and studying your Bible reveals its value. The only way to know what God wants for you is to know Him. You must spend time getting to know Him by reading His word.

Think of someone in your life that you know very well—your spouse, parent, child, best friend, or anyone with whom you have a close relationship. Because you have spent a significant amount of time with that person, you've learned what makes them happy, what upsets them, their character traits, and how you bring value to their lives. You've learned the things you can do to please them. And you've also learned what not to do, so as to avoid hurting them.

It's the same way with God. When you know Him, you have an inner sense of what pleases Him. You become familiar with His character and learn how to pray for what brings glory to Him. You know, instinctively, what God doesn't want for you because of His character. In time you learn how to align your will with His.

... With Right Motives

Now our lesson on prayer gets real good. James 4:2 teaches us that we don't have what we want because we don't ask God. And when we do ask, we don't receive, because our motives are all wrong.

For example, let's say I asked God to help me write this book because I want to become famous. Asking for help to write the book is a good thing, as God wants me to depend on Him to carry out anything that brings glory and honor to Him. But asking for His help because I want to become famous shifts the attention from God to me. When the intentions of my heart don't align with His, I shouldn't expect to receive His blessings.

. . . And Believe

Finally, this last part brings many to a screeching halt. If you can get through the first three—ask, in His will, with the right motives—it is usually at this next point where most of us fall short. We are encouraged in James 1:6–8 to believe and not doubt. The Bible says anyone who doubts is unstable, double-minded, and shouldn't expect to receive anything from God. I have found that the best way for me to believe what I'm praying for is to make sure that the first three components are in place. If I'm asking for that which is already in His will, with the right motives, it's a win/win.

Lord knows I've missed this last one many times. How about you? Did you score four out of four? If not, check yourself the next time you enter your prayer time asking God for the desires of your heart. Make sure that you ask for that which is in His will, with the right motives, while believing with all your heart that you'll receive what you've asked.

I know what you're thinking. "But wait a minute, Anita. You asked God for a miracle, to save your husband's life, but he died." Yes, I know. I believe God to be a miracle worker, but it was not in His will to keep Cecil here on this earth. My motives were for my husband to remain with me and I believed it could happen. Remember, the day before the doctor announced hospice for my husband, I prayed and told God I would accept His will. My husband's spirit is at rest, and when Jesus returns, he will be raised to life. That's the miracle God offered, and for that reason, I have peace. I prayed for my husband's healing. God actually did answer my prayer. Cecil is healed in eternity, in the name of Jesus. God's answers to prayer will not always come in the form that we desire, and that is according to His wisdom. I would much rather my husband be resting in peace with the miracle of eternal life than suffering here on Earth with me.

Chapter 14

Worship

The final item in our LPK is worship. What's the first thing that comes to mind when you hear the word *worship*? The visual of singing along with a choir or worship team in church? Others may think of going to church and being a part of different ministries. While both are acts of worship, neither one alone defines worship.

Worship should be a lifestyle, not a single act. It's not merely something you do on Sunday morning. It's an outpouring of adoration for God that manifests itself in your daily living.

Worship is honoring God's Word with your life. It's your heart's response to knowing Him. It's uplifting Him in the presence of others, outside of the church, sharing His Word. Worship expresses itself as you treasure Him by spending time alone in His presence, enjoying Him, and being satisfied in Him.

Confining worship to a single day of the week does a great disservice to the ministry of Jesus Christ in your life. You see, it's quite easy to worship God in church while surrounded by like-minded believers. But it's entirely different when you step outside those doors to face the world. In order for God to be truly glorified in you, worship Him in all areas of your life.

Worship at Home

Your family is your first ministry to God. Taking care of home and allowing God to use you to nurture the ones you're closest with is an act of worship.

Worship at Work

How you show up in your workplace says a lot about who you are as a person. Being present and honest and fulfilling your assignments without compromising your faith is an act of worship.

Worship at School

Applying yourself to knowledge and using what you learn to help you better serve the people God has placed along your path in life is an act of worship, when done with integrity.

Worship at Play

Engaging in activities outside of work and school that uphold your godly morals as a child of God is also an act of worship.

Be sure that you don't isolate worship to a single act or day of the week or area of your life. Allow worship to be a lifestyle. Honor God in your home, work, school, and play, so that others will take notice of His Light and be drawn to Him.

Now that you've been equipped with the necessary tools for your Life Preparedness Kit, let's apply these to your daily life.

In order to STAND in the midst of a devastating life trial, you must be prepared ahead of time. You prepare yourself by becoming deeply rooted in Christ. Becoming deeply rooted requires that you do the work.

You must have a SAVING **FAITH** (believe in Jesus). Your saving faith activates living faith, which is apportioned to you as God determines, to be used in your daily life.

You must fulfill God's **PURPOSE** in your life, which is to glorify Him. As you're living His purpose, He will call you to different assignments in different seasons of life, at which times you will exercise the gifts and talents He's blessed you with, all for the purpose of blessing other people.

The **BIBLE** will be your roadmap to help you navigate through the life He has designed for you, providing you with the information and tools you need along the way.

PRAYER will draw you close to Him and provide you guidance, through the Holy Spirit, as you pray and listen.

Finally, **WORSHIP** will help you to elevate Jesus, making Him of utmost importance, while living to honor Him in every area of your life.

Keeping these five items active in your daily living will help you to become deeply rooted in Christ. Then, when you come face to face with a life storm, you will have a firm foundation upon which to STAND.

Becoming a deeply rooted believer doesn't happen overnight. It's a process, a lifelong journey that you must pursue for yourself. No Pastor, Bible Study Leader, Seminary Instructor, parent, or friend will be able to do this work for you. God makes Himself available to you. Now all you have to do is grab His hand and walk along. Because He has your best interest in mind, you can trust Him.

Part 3

TRUST

"Trust in the Lord with all your heart
and lean not on your own understanding;
in all your ways submit to him, and
he will make your paths straight."

(Proverbs 3:5–6)

Chapter 15

Sovereignty of God

G od is Sovereign! Thinking about the trial you may be facing now or storms that you've experienced in the past, how does it make you feel when you hear this phrase? Do you have a clear understanding of what *sovereign* means? For some, this is one of those churchy words that pastors and church folks throw around all the time. The word was foreign to me when I first started learning about God, so let's talk about it. What is the sovereignty of God?

Google defines the word *sovereign* as follows:

> "(noun) a supreme ruler, especially a monarch; (adjective) possessing supreme or ultimate power."

God, the Creator of heaven and earth, is the Supreme Ruler of all He has created. To make it short and simple, whenever someone says, "God is Sovereign," they mean God is in control. He woke you up this morning and provides the air you're breathing right now.

As you're learning how to STAND in your faith by becoming deeply rooted in Christ, you will also learn to TRUST the sovereignty of God when faced with a devastating life trial.

Anything that God does and allows has purpose. He's an intentional God. Everything good that happens in your life, anything that has eternal value, is from God, even down to the smallest details. And here's the hard part: anything bad that has happened in your life has been allowed by God. Absolutely nothing can enter into your life without God knowing about it.

This second part is a very difficult reality to grasp, and I realize there may be some terrible, evil, and unspeakable things that have happened to you, things that may be happening right now.

I wish I could tell you that I understand why God allows such devastation, but I don't. All I know is that when sin entered the world through Adam and Eve, it opened the door for pain and suffering. Again, if you didn't read the gospel message in Chapter 5, please stop reading right now and go back to that chapter so you will understand about God's wrath. Because of that first sin that took place in the Garden of Eden, God sometimes allows horrible things to happen to His own people.

For example, have you heard of Job?

If you haven't, you can read the full story in the Book of Job from your Bible, but I'll give you a short summary. Job was described as an upright man, and God said there was none other like him. Yet God still gave Satan permission to inflict multiple tragedies upon Job's life until Job lost almost everything. He lost his possessions. His children were murdered. His body was attacked with painful boils and sores. The only thing God would not allow Satan to do was kill him. Job had to endure the affliction. Then, after it was all done, God restored Job's life back to better than it was before.

As difficult as it is to hear that Jesus allows tragedies in your life, here's a truth from the Bible I want you to capture and embrace:

"Jesus Christ is the same yesterday and today and forever." (Hebrews 13:8)

Therefore, God still has the power to restore you from the devastation of your trials—the same way He restored Job to a greater life.

God Always Provides

The Bible says to "Trust in the Lord with all your heart and lean not on your own understanding; in all your ways submit to him, and he will make your paths straight" (Proverbs 3:5–6).

When you trust and acknowledge Him in the midst of your trial—whatever you're going through—God will direct your steps along the path. He will provide what you need to make it through. He will also go above and beyond, revealing His presence and power within that provision.

Time after time, God sent exactly what we needed during my husband's illness. I had this incredible sense of expectancy when I prayed about the different things we were dealing with, because I knew He would take care of us. There were some situations that were out of the ordinary, but I didn't know that at the time. All I knew was that we were in need, and God would provide in His own way—that was enough for me. All I needed was the peace of God, and that came by trusting Him.

I have so many stories of how God provided for our needs in miraculous ways during that time, but the one that sticks out in my mind the most is when Cecil was in the hospital and needed to be transported to City of Hope for radiation treatment.

The day after his first radiation treatment, Cecil woke up at home with a headache and was very confused. I got him dressed and set him in front of the TV in his wheelchair. When I looked back at him, his eyes were moving in every direction, his face was twitching, and he was talking to the TV, but what he was saying didn't match what was happening on the screen. Then all of a sudden, he turned his head to the left as far as it would go and stared. I called his name several times, but he was unresponsive. I tapped his leg—still no response. I grabbed his face to turn it towards me, but I couldn't move it. It was as if his head was stuck in that position. I grabbed my phone and called 911. The paramedics came, determined he had suffered a focal seizure, and took him to the ER.

On the way to the hospital, I rode in the back of the ambulance with my husband, and I remember saying over and over, "God, please help my husband. Please protect him. Please heal him."

After running a couple of tests, the doctor determined that his steroid dose needed to be increased so that his body could endure the radiation. They stabilized and discharged him to go home that evening and told me what to look for and when to call, should the seizures return.

The next day, the seizures started up again. I called the paramedics, and they took him back to the emergency room. He was admitted into the hospital this time because the seizures continued while he was in the ER. His neurosurgeon ordered another MRI on his brain, and the scan revealed that his condition had progressed into the most aggressive form of brain cancer, glioblastoma multiforme, so they decided to treat it aggressively.

This time the doctor kept him at the hospital to see how his body would respond to the next radiation treatment. I was so grateful; I didn't want to take him home in that condition.

In order to receive radiation treatment, he needed to be transported from the hospital to City of Hope (COH) down the street—which meant we would need an ambulance transport. While we waited for him to be stabilized, the caseworker went to work contacting our insurance company to see if the transport was covered under our plan.

Before we could get a response from the insurance company, we received word that he was being transported by ambulance to his radiation treatments for the next two days, courtesy of COH.

Those two treatments went well, and afterward we received word that COH would continue to transport him to radiation for the duration of his stay in the hospital.

When the time came for him to be discharged, I was a bit concerned. Cecil still wasn't able to walk on his own, and he wasn't done with his radiation treatments—which meant I would be on my own transporting him from our home to COH. There was no way I'd be able to get him into the car, and the caseworker informed me that ambulance transports weren't covered under our insurance plan.

Therefore, I contacted our representative from the Los Angeles Firemen's Relief Association (LAFRA) and asked for help. (LAFRA is a resource within the LAFD that supports its members in times of need.) We received approval for Cecil to be transported from our home to COH every day until November 12, 2017.

God is Sovereign! When circumstances seem out of your control, trust that He is working all things out.

Cecil's ambulance transports to COH were scheduled to end November 12, but his radiation treatments weren't over by that point. I started looking at other options and was ready to make it work somehow.

We were able to work with our youngest son's schedule so he could be home to help me take his dad to radiation in my car each day, except

Wednesdays. Cool. That meant I only needed outside help one day each week.

But before that could happen, my son came back to say he got hired for a second job, so he wouldn't be able to help me with Cecil. I didn't want my son to feel bad about accepting the job; after all, at the beginning of this journey, we told our sons to continue living their lives. I congratulated him, told him how proud I was, and that I would work it out.

In reality, I had no idea what I was going to do. I started working on a Plan B and made a list of all the men I could call to come help me get my husband to COH. Then I planned to make a schedule so that someone would be there every day of the week to help.

However, later that day, I received a call informing me that Cecil's transports to COH had been approved for the remainder of his treatments. I gasped and praised God. I didn't even ask for that, but God knew what I needed.

God is a provider. I knew He would help us. I saw what He had been doing throughout our journey thus far, and I knew He would continue to provide. So, while I was working on my Plan B, God came through with His Plan A.

When you're going through a trial, it's easy to look at the circumstances and try to figure everything out on your own. However, God is available and willing to take the weight off your shoulders. You can trust Him with your trials, and when you do, you will reap the benefits.

Chapter 16

Three Benefits of Trusting God

Have you ever heard these phrases? "Leave room for God." "Get out of God's way." "God doesn't need your help." There have been moments in my life when I tried so hard to fix problems that I left no room for God to move in the situations. Can you relate?

Early in my life, I developed a controlling personality. Needless to say, that caused some issues in my marriage, and it created tension with my sons in their teenage years. And, unknowingly, I was doing internal damage to myself. Trying to control everything is a heavy burden to carry.

I had to learn to make room for God. For my family's health, I had to let go of my controlling ways and let God take the reins. It was a struggle in the beginning, but then something beautiful happened. In letting go, I received peace of mind. Not a bad tradeoff!

By the time my husband was diagnosed with brain cancer, I'd already had a good amount of practice in letting go. In the midst of the chaos and uncertainty of Cecil's illness, I experienced peace that helped guide my perspective of what was happening. In turn, others were also able to witness the power of God at work.

This choice to trust God is a lifelong endeavor. I'm by no means perfect in this area, but with God's help I continue to hold tightly to trust. The benefits are priceless. When you allow yourself to trust God, making room for Him to move in your situation, He will grant you peace of mind, a godly perspective, and a powerful witness—and others who see this in your life will be encouraged. Let's take a look at these three benefits of trusting God.

Peace of Mind

Worry is the thief that robs you of peace. Jesus tells us not to worry. He knows exactly what you need and makes provisions for that in His perfect wisdom. He says that when you focus on seeking His kingdom, all other things will be given to you as well (Matthew 6:33).

Therein lies the key to peace: focusing on His kingdom. But what does that mean? What is His kingdom? For many years, I thought of the Kingdom of God as a place, like Heaven. But I've since learned that His kingdom is His reign. He reigns in all authority and is in control of all things. So, when Jesus tells us to seek His kingdom, He's saying that we are to desire and surrender to His rule over our lives.

When your focus is in the right place—seeking His kingdom, accepting His Lordship over your life—it's much easier to recognize when He's providing for your needs and answering prayers.

In contrast, if you're focusing on the problem instead of the Problem Solver, it's very possible that God is providing for your needs but you aren't recognizing it. Rather than worrying about what could happen in the situation or what's not happening, put your trust in the Sovereign God who knows the end from the beginning.

When you worry, you impose upon yourself that which belongs to God. For many of us, worry is our default. When something goes wrong, instead of turning to prayer and praise, we choose worry and fear.

Full transparency: there were times during my husband's illness when I chose fear first. In those instances, I couldn't feel peace—His peace—until I surrendered and focused on Jesus. And as the Bible says, His peace surpasses all understanding (Philippians 4:7).

In John 14:27, Jesus promised to give us peace and told us not to worry because He doesn't give to us as the world gives. The peace that Jesus gives is internal and comes as we rest in the certainty that God is Sovereign. The peace offered by the world is external and usually based upon financial security, education, career status, material possessions, etc. Scripture is what you use to combat worry and fear, which is why planting God's Word in your heart, through the memorization of scripture, is so important. When you speak God's Word into the worry and fear, the tradeoff is life and peace.

Godly Perspective

When my husband was scheduled to have his first surgery on my fifty-first birthday—and his second on our twenty-second wedding anniversary—I embraced those dates as opportunities to save his life. I never felt sad or viewed it as an inconvenience. I was hopeful and grateful because I truly believed that God would perform a miracle and heal him from the cancer.

God didn't heal Cecil here on this Earth. Although He allowed my husband to die from brain cancer, I developed a deeper trust in God. As a result, He provided me with a supernatural, overwhelming peace, which drew me even closer to Him. It strengthened my faith and gave me a whole new perspective on life.

One of the most common questions people ask during a life trial is, "Why? Why is this happening to me?" I get it—when I looked at our situation, I didn't understand, either. But not once did I ask God, "Why?" Instead, when that thought came, I always said to myself, "Why *not* him? Why *not* our family?" Before Cecil was diagnosed with brain cancer, there were many who went before him, and unfortunately people are still being diagnosed with brain cancer.

The God we serve is no respecter of persons. That means He doesn't play favorites. Contrary to what others may want to believe, being a follower of Jesus Christ doesn't guarantee a trouble-free life. In fact, Jesus promised that we would have trouble.

"In this world you will have trouble. But take heart! I have overcome the world." (John 16:33)

When you trust God in the midst of your trial, He will help you to see things through a different lens. Embracing a Godly perspective doesn't cancel out the pain and difficulty of your circumstances, but it does help you view what's happening in light of your belief that God is in control. Therefore, instead of complaining, you choose to trust that God is working in the midst of the trial. You are reminded that God is Sovereign. Don't forget His promise to you that "in all things God works for the good of those who love Him, who have been called according to His purpose" (Romans 8:28).

The way you respond to any trial in life is largely dependent upon the perspective you choose to embrace. When you know that God is in control, your perspective will align with that truth, and your actions will represent that perspective. Then others will see His Light shining through your example, providing a powerful witness for Christ.

Powerful Witness

When you choose to trust God in the midst of your trials, you begin to behave in a way that honors Him and allows His light to shine and draw others to Him.

Whether you believe it or not, someone is always watching you, especially when you're going through a trial. The question to consider is, what are they watching you do? When they see you persevering through your trials, you're demonstrating what's possible through Jesus.

To be perfectly clear, I'm not saying that you need to "put on a show" or behave in a certain way because people are watching. What I am saying is that when you put your trust in God during your trial, He illuminates Himself through you. I call it the Shine. Some people will recognize it and others will have no clue. Some will think it's you that they're drawn to, but it's actually the Light of Jesus that attracts them.

With my husband's permission, I went public with our news about his diagnosis. I wanted as many people praying with us as possible, so I started sharing our journey.

While my motive was to have a community of people praying with us, it went far beyond my expectations. I started receiving comments from others about how the messages I shared encouraged and inspired them.

As I shared our journey, I included how I was feeling, and how God was working through the circumstances.

After my husband took his last breath, I continued to share my heart. I shared the pain and suffering as I experienced it. I shared the breakthroughs and setbacks. Through it all, I continued to praise God and reminded people how good He is. I was completely blown away when I realized that God was using the most devastating time in my life to encourage others. Of course, I had seen this happen with other people. However, I never imagined God would use me in that way. I never thought I would make an impact on another person's heart with my story.

God has the power to use your pain and suffering to help other people. I'm not repeating something I've heard. This has been my experience. I'm living this truth. The trials you experience in life are not for you only, nor are they in vain. Because God is purposeful and intentional, when you walk in the light as He is in the light, those around you will be exposed to that light as well. You can't control it, and neither can they.

Jesus said that you're the light of the world (Matthew 5:14). So, when you trust God in the midst of your devastating trial, He causes His light to reach other people as they go through their own stuff.

At this point, you may be thinking: "Okay, Anita, I get it. Trusting God is beneficial to me because it gives me peace of mind, a godly perspective, and a powerful witness. But how do I do that? How do I trust God?"

Chapter 17

How to Trust God
in the Trial

I know it's easy for me to say, "Trust God," when I'm not walking in your shoes. I understand that it's hard to focus when everything around you seems to be falling apart. And I realize it may be difficult to trust God when He's the one who allows devastation into your life. So how is this possible? How do you trust Him to carry you through? These are valid questions, but if you will remember three things and take one more STEP, I believe you will see that it's possible.

Remember God's Sovereignty

Remember, God is in control! No matter what the situation looks like, no matter how you feel, no matter what anyone says, God doesn't make mistakes. He orchestrates all things to His glory. He sees what you're going through. He knows and cares about every detail of your life. You may not feel like He's in control sometimes, but He says this to you:

> *"Be still and know that I am God; I will be exalted among the nations, I will be exalted in the earth." (Psalm 46:10)*

So, hold on and remember who God is.

Remember the Evidence

Do you have evidence of God providing for your needs in the past? Do you have mental records of God's provision in your life? Were there times when He blessed you in ways you didn't expect? Has He ever answered a prayer that you've prayed? Does He provide for your daily needs in life? Maybe you can remember a time when God swept you off your feet with His presence and provision.

When the weight of your situation is so heavy that you can barely see a way out, remember what He has done for you in the past.

"I will remember the deeds of the Lord; yes, I will remember your miracles of long ago. I will consider all your works and meditate on all your mighty deeds" (Psalm 77:11–12).

Recall the many blessings and allow them to encourage you to believe that He will come through again, in His own time.

Remember God's Promises

The Word of God is full of many promises He has made to His people. When you embrace His promises, you open the way for trust. Here is yet another reason why reading the Bible is so important. He speaks directly to you about all that awaits you by way of His promises. Remember what He has said.

While all His promises are important, the one I encourage you to hold close to your heart when you're in the midst of your storm says, *"He will never leave you nor forsake you"* (Deuteronomy 31:6).

Knowing that He promises to be with you should bring comfort and peace. This promise is repeated throughout the Bible to many different people. And remember, God is no respecter of persons, so this promise applies to you too!

Wait on the Lord

Now, after remembering these things, you need to act. Waiting on the Lord to provide for your needs should not be a passive waiting. It's moving forward and acting as if the blessing is already on the way. It's acting as if you already know He's coming through for you. It's being intentional about your actions as you wait for Him to show up, in His own way. It's being confident in His promised provision.

There's a story in the Bible about a guy named Jeremiah who wrote a letter to God's people after they had been carried off into exile. In this letter, God said they were to continue living, working, building families, praying, and prospering, all while they were in captivity. He said that He would bring them out and bless them.

He didn't write in any provision for complaining, no provision for feeling sorry for themselves, no provision for running away. Rather, He told them to "seek peace and prosperity" right where they were—in captivity (Jeremiah 29:7)! He basically told them to thrive while waiting on Him.

Remember, God doesn't change. He remains the same. What He promised to the exiles, He also promises to us. But how do you wait on Him today, in a different time? How do you wait on the Lord in the midst of your trial? You wait the same way, by thriving and waiting for Him to bring you out.

Thriving in the midst of a trial isn't the same for everyone. For some, the situation is so heavy that getting out of bed, taking a shower, and getting dressed is a huge feat. It's okay. Thrive where you are. For others, releasing steam by running and exercising to keep their minds and bodies healthy is more of a challenge than it was before, but they do it anyway. This is what thriving looks like, tailored to their specific circumstance. Many find it difficult to pray when they have so much turmoil in their lives, but they simply get with God and say whatever they're feeling. That's thriving! There are also those who make significant changes in their lives or accomplish incredible tasks or assignments from God in the midst of their trials. This, too, is thriving! It doesn't matter the size of the task. Thriving is continuing to engage with life, one day at a time, one step at a time, one breath at a time. God gives you permission to seek peace and prosperity in the midst of your trial.

When I was caring for my husband, peace in itself was all the prosperity I needed. Many believe that prosperity is associated only with money and other material possessions. I believe that prosperity is different for every person, based upon the circumstances in which you're living. God increased my peace of mind in a way that I couldn't explain. And it came at a time when there should have been no peace, according to the world's standards. I didn't have to wait for my husband to be healed to have peace. It was given to me in the midst of the waiting, as I trusted God. No amount of money can buy peace of mind amid a devastating life trial.

So how do you wait on the Lord? By living, praying, praising, and expecting His provision.

If you TRUST God in the midst of your trial, He will give you peace of mind, a godly perspective, and a powerful witness.

You learn to TRUST Him by remembering that He is sovereign over all things, by remembering the evidence of His provisions in the past, by remembering His promises to you, and finally, by waiting on him with expectancy.

By standing and trusting in the midst of your trial, something else happens simultaneously. You build endurance. You position yourself to endure the trial.

Part 4

ENDURE

"Consider it pure joy, my brothers and sisters,
whenever you face trials of many kinds,
because you know that the testing of your
faith produces perseverance. Let perseverance
finish its work so that you may be mature
and complete, not lacking anything."

(James 1:2–4)

Chapter 18

What Does It Mean to Endure with Grace?

I f I told you that, with grace, you're capable of enduring any trial that God allows into your life, would you believe me? Here is how Google defines *endure*.

> *"To hold up under (pain, etc.); to tolerate; to continue; to bear pain, etc. without flinching."*

If you were faced with the worst trial imaginable, do you think you could hold up under it without flinching? Given what I've experienced, I can't imagine going through it without flinching. Sometimes enduring the trial involves a lot of flinching. Endurance is found in the staying power, not the lack of flinching.

I should explain what I mean by "endure with grace," but first, let's talk about what it doesn't mean. Enduring with grace doesn't mean you have to be perfect in the way you deal with your trial. It doesn't mean you're not allowed to express your emotions. It doesn't mean you will always feel okay, and it certainly doesn't mean you will always know what to say or do. And finally, it doesn't mean that you're not allowed to cry. Not everyone is comfortable with expressing pain or grief through tears. However, if you find yourself crying through your trial, please understand that it's not a sign of weakness. Whenever you cry, embrace it as a moment of cleansing.

When Cecil died, there were nights when I would lie in my bed, curled up in the fetal position, crying until my head throbbed with pain. There were episodes of screaming and pounding on whatever was near me—the floor, sofa, counter, or whatever. This doesn't sound very graceful, does it? But, after each episode, I felt better and refreshed. That's the cleansing power of tears.

While making myself a fruit salad one morning, I thought about how I used to prepare his meals as he lay in his sickbed, watching me from across the room. I thought I was home alone, and started screaming and crying, my heart burning with pain. I wanted to touch him again, to give him another plate of food. I wanted to wash his face and play his favorite music for him. I thought, "If only I could have him back, to say 'I love you' one more time. If only I had lain in his sickbed with him before he died." Excruciating pain pulsed through my heart and warm tears poured down my face, as I bent over, holding onto the counter for support. Painful sobs filled the entire house, and I could barely breathe as my nose became clogged and runny.

All of a sudden, I heard footsteps racing down the stairs. Then Jordon yelled out, "Mom!" He grabbed me, removed the knife from my hand—that I didn't even realize I was still holding—and walked me over to the sofa. He held me as I sat there, sobbing. I wanted the pain to stop, but I had to endure this part of the grief process many times. The cleansing was taking place. This is part of enduring with grace. It's about being present and allowing the process to take its course without running away, without hiding.

If you try to be perfect while enduring, you deny yourself the healing and restoration through the authentic experience. When I say "endure with grace," I'm encouraging you to humble yourself to the reality of what you're facing. Allow God to walk you through the journey without fighting—there are some things you simply can't change. Enduring with grace is about following God's lead as He directs your steps along the journey. It's doing the necessary work that leads to discovery. It's thriving in the midst of your storm. And remember, thriving involves baby steps for some and huge leaps for others.

Before moving any further into this conversation, I need to bring up the topic of abuse. You should never remain in an abusive environment for the sake of endurance. That's not what I'm talking about here. There are some circumstances that require help from law enforcement or other outside help. If you are currently in a situation where you're being abused, in any way, you MUST seek help, now. I know you may be afraid to reach out for fear of retaliation from your abuser. You've probably been told that you or your family members will be harmed if you speak up, or that you'll lose your job or career, or that nobody cares about you. Understand that these are brainwashing tactics that perpetrators of abuse use to silence their victims. I am not an expert on abuse, nor do I claim to know all the workings of the abuser's mind. But remember the abuse I witnessed in my own home as a child. And again, when abuse is present, law enforcement needs to be involved.

If you are indeed experiencing abuse in your life at this time, stop reading right now and turn to the Resources section in the back of this book. I have compiled a list of hotline phone numbers to call for help. I pray that you will find strength and courage in saying "NO MORE" to the abuse, by taking that first step to saving your life and perhaps the lives of others.

Again, enduring the trial with grace means you're allowing God to walk you through it, while taking whatever actions are necessary to improve and thrive. If you're in an abusive relationship, do what you need to remove yourself from danger. If you are ill, follow your doctor's advice to improve your health. If you struggle with substance abuse, find a support group for accountability. No matter what trial you're facing, God will lead you and provide opportunities for healing, support, improvement or whatever you need.

Seven Ways to Endure the Trial

As I mentioned before, enduring with grace is more than just waiting—it involves living and thriving in the midst of the storm. It's one thing to say that, but what does it really look like? I've created a list of seven things that helped me to endure my trial with grace. Some of these were habits I'd already developed but needed to tweak during this season of endurance, and others were habits I had to learn along the way. A few tips were advice I received from family, friends, and even strangers. Some of these practices came easily, while others were a real struggle for me in those circumstances. Many of the tips will probably be common sense to you, but there may also be a few lightbulb moments. Whatever the case, listen and take mental notes because something in this chapter may be helpful to you during your trial as well.

1. Remember Who You Are in Christ

While I was walking along this journey with Cecil, these are some of the comments I heard:

"I don't know how you do it. I couldn't be that strong."

"I could never go through that and handle it so well."

"I hope that I can be that strong if something happens to my husband."

"Your husband is lucky. I would be of no help to mine."

That last one made me laugh. One day I was thinking about these comments and wondered why God was allowing me to hear these things. My sinful temptation would lead me to think that I'm somebody special. While I know I'm called by God and He has planted His love inside of me to pour out onto others, I don't want to be that person who seeks attention for myself. If God isn't being glorified, and the Light of Jesus isn't being illuminated as I serve, then something isn't right.

I kept pondering and asked myself, "Why is this happening? Why are people telling me these things?" The only answer I received in my spirit was, "So that you will believe." I didn't get it. What was I supposed to believe? That I was strong? Then it finally clicked. You see, in some areas of our lives, we have no problem believing we are who God says we are. If it's familiar, we're good and find it easy to move forward with Christ as our banner. But when we end up in uncomfortable and unfamiliar circumstances, we become reluctant to hold to the same beliefs about our identity. Our confidence in who we are begins to waver.

I think we do this because we're focusing on our own finite abilities. When all we can see is our own shortcomings, we're not considering the infinite power of God. The Bible tells us that all things are possible with God (Matthew 19:26). And I've learned that "You never know how strong you are until being strong is the only choice you have."[2] This quote is inscribed on a little box—given to me by a dear friend—that I keep in a place where I can see it every morning. I believe God sent people to remind me because I needed to hear it in the midst of the trial. Every time someone made that comment, I would either respond or think in my mind, "Jesus is my strength."

As you're STANDING in your faith and TRUSTING the sovereignty of God, He will help you to ENDURE the trial by reminding you of who you are. Sometimes He will send other people to deliver that reminder over and over again. When the storm hits, if you believe what He says about you, then you will rise to the occasion of endurance.

Do you know who you are? The scriptures are filled with descriptive words about your identity in Christ. He says you are:

- Chosen (1 Peter 2:9)
- A child of God (Romans 8:16)
- A royal priesthood (1 Peter 2:9)
- Forgiven (Colossians 1:13–14)
- Justified (Romans 5:1)
- Sanctified (1 Corinthians 6:11)
- God's workmanship (Ephesians 2:10)
- God's servant (1 Corinthians 3:9)
- Christ's friend (John 15:15)
- An heir of God (Romans 8:17)
- An overcomer (1 John 4:4)
- An imitator of Jesus (Ephesians 5:1)
- More than a conqueror (Romans 8:37)
- A new creation (2 Corinthians 5:17)
- The light of the world (Matthew 5:14)
- The salt of the earth (Matthew 5:13)
- Strong in the Lord (Ephesians 6:10)
- A laborer with Christ (1 Corinthians 3:9)
- Blessed coming in and going out (Deuteronomy 28:6)

---

2. Vincent Thnay, *Quote Worthy* (N.p.: Lulu.com, 2015).

In order to endure the trial in a way that glorifies God, you must believe that you are who He says you are and live accordingly. Be empowered by your identity—because when you are, your actions glorify God. Your endurance will only go as far as your belief. Remember who you are.

2. Pray

As you know, prayer is a way of life and an important part of the Life Preparedness Kit. However, it's important to briefly bring it up again because when you're encountering the day-to-day events that accompany trials, you may need an extra prayer or more to help you throughout the day. There is absolutely no limit to the number of times you can pray in a single day. God welcomes you with open arms.

Another thing to consider is that you may encounter moments when you simply don't know what to pray. At times during my husband's illness, the energy was completely sucked out of me. Times when all I could say was, "God, help!" Times when all I had inside of me was, "Jesus!" That was my prayer when I felt depleted, and it was enough for God.

When you're at a loss for words, your prayers don't need to be anything other than what's on your heart. He already knows, so you don't need to force anything.

Also, remember that the Spirit himself intercedes for you through wordless groans when you're at a loss of what to say. He rewards a heart that is surrendered to Him. If all you can do is fall to your knees in silence, He accepts you as you are.

"In the same way, the Spirit helps us in our weakness. We do not know what we ought to pray for, but the Spirit himself intercedes for us through wordless groans. And he who searches our hearts knows the mind of the Spirit, because the Spirit intercedes for God's people in accordance with the will of God." (Romans 8:26–27)

3. Resist the Enemy

I'm pretty sure you've heard the saying, "When it rains, it pours," right? When you're in the midst of a trial, the rest of life doesn't stop happening so that you can deal with your storm. I won't tell you that everything bad that happens in your life is from the devil; I don't believe that. However, I do believe there is an evil force at work in the spiritual realm, who is the devil. And if you are seeking to honor God by enduring the trials of life, the enemy is nearby, looking for an opportunity to take you off course, to break you down, to wear you out and cause you to give up. He doesn't want others to witness you giving glory to and praising God through your storm because that attributes power to God. If he can trip you up and cause you to go left instead of right, if he can redirect your focus to something that gets your blood boiling and curls your hands into fists, he will stop at nothing to achieve his purpose.

Satan's purpose is to render you ineffective in your praise and witness—that's his job. So, instead of getting mad at him for doing his job, get rooted in the Word of God so that you will know how to fight back. Get your feet planted on a solid foundation, and when the attack comes, you'll be able to recognize its origin. My family had the unfortunate opportunity of witnessing one of these attacks in our home during my husband's illness.

Before I get into the story, let me be totally transparent with you. I need to give you some background information first, so you will understand how I went from sweet little church lady to hardcore Rambo chick in this incident. There's a girl living inside of me and her name is Nee-Nee. She is straight from the 'hood and doesn't think before she reacts. I grew up in South Central Los Angeles, and you learn to have tough skin growing up in the inner city. You know that I got into fights on the way to church as a little girl. When I was older, I always tried to carry myself like a classy young lady, but I wasn't one to take crap from people. Class went straight out the window when I used to tell people off. One time this got me into a car chase with my best friend—we started out being the chasers, but our victims turned on us and sent us off speeding and screaming through the streets. Whew! I was a mess sometimes, but I was still a lady.

Go ahead and laugh! I didn't walk around in fear, nor was I a bad person, but I learned how to protect and stand up for myself in every way.

As I've matured over the years and learned how God wants me to respond, I've kept Nee-Nee on lockdown. But every once in a while, she peeks her head out to see if she needs to make an appearance. And sometimes she does, like that day at the gym. God knows that I am still a work in progress. I have not arrived, and I don't always meet His standards of obedience. The God I serve knows my weaknesses, though, and when I confess my sins to Him, He forgives me every time I mess up. I'm not proud of my misbehavior, but I'm forgiven. I'm not perfect in this life, but I'm His. Now, let me give you an example of how the enemy will sneak in and try to ruin your praise and worship to God in the midst of a life trial.

On August 27, 2017, twenty days after my husband's diagnosis, it was a beautiful day for our family, and everything was going so well. I was on schedule with all of Cecil's medications. My friend, who's a physical therapist, came over to work with Cecil to get him back on his feet. A couple from church brought over a lovely dinner and visited with us for a while. Later that evening, we went to visit our friends, just to get Cecil out of the house for a change of atmosphere.

Shortly after we arrived home, all hell broke loose. The enemy raised his head and an ugly crisis followed. I was upstairs changing into my nightclothes when all of a sudden I heard yelling. I thought maybe there was excitement over something on television, so I ignored it. But the loud voices continued, so I paused to listen. It was then that I realized those were angry voices coming from my house, not the television.

As quickly as I could, I rushed down the hallway, still dressing myself on the way, and ran downstairs into the family room. There I found my husband and son in an argument, my son yelling at my husband. I couldn't believe my eyes or ears. My husband tried to get up from the sofa, but he fell back down because he couldn't keep his balance. The look of anger and hurt was fixed on his face. Heat began to rise from the pit of my stomach, rushing to my face. Unlock the key, remove the chain, release the bar, and Nee-Nee emerges! Without asking any questions, I stormed into that room, as my hands formed into fists. I got into my son's face, pointing my finger and yelling, "Don't you EVER yell at my husband again! And how DARE you talk to your dad that way and disrespect him! GET OUT! You get out of our house right now and you'd better not come back!"

The rage inside of me was so intense that I started shaking my head, forming fists again, looking back and forth from my husband to my son. I wanted to start swinging on my son. I wanted to sock him everywhere, but I managed to restrain myself because I didn't want to upset my husband any further. I was so angry as I looked over at my husband and saw him sitting there, unable to do anything. I know he wanted to be the one to discipline our son, but he couldn't move. Maybe it was better—Cecil would have taken my son to the ground. And who knows how that would have affected his condition, both physically and emotionally.

This was a case of the enemy coming in to disrupt peace in the midst of the storm. Since there was so much love being poured into us that day from other people, he decided to attack from within the family. But then, God! He is so perfect in His ways.

He set it up for my mama to be there that evening. Yes, my mother witnessed all the ugliness. After the commotion settled, she walked into the room and said, "Can we just pray?" As tears filled my eyes, my mother and I stood over Cecil and began to pray. I told God how angry I was and how much I wanted to lay hands on that boy. I asked God to help me.

As we continued praying and praising, I began to feel a different wave of heat move through my body and the peace of God hovering over me. As the tears began to fall, a feeling of weakness and calm overcame my body. It was the most amazing experience.

What I didn't realize is that our son was upstairs calling out for help at the same time. God sent him an angel, and she told him what he needed to do. After a while, he joined us downstairs and apologized to his dad. We all talked and made peace with each other, and I allowed my son to stay in the house.

The Bible says to resist the enemy and he will flee from you (see James 4:7). You resist the enemy by speaking God's word and praying. As soon as you recognize an attack is in motion, start speaking the scriptures and calling out God's name. The devil can't stand that, and he will flee.

4. Breathe

The enemy's favorite playground is your mind. His strategy is to make you think all kinds of negative things about yourself, your circumstances, and everybody around you. If he succeeds, then his job is done. At this point, he doesn't need to pursue you anymore, because the negative thinking will lead you to the dark places where he resides.

Every action begins with a thought. Negative thoughts give way to negative words, which often lead to behaviors that are not pleasing to God. When you're in the midst of a trial and all the things associated with the storm are weighing down on you, the negative thoughts will come. You have a choice to make at this point.

My husband's cousin gave me a treasured piece of advice that completely enhanced my way of dealing with negative thoughts. He said, "Whenever a negative thought enters your mind, stop, slow your breathing, and concentrate on the breathing." And it works!

The first time I tried this technique was during one of my husband's hospital stays. As I was visiting, I began to feel the weight of everything happening to him. I remember walking down the hallway to take a break from the room. I needed fresh air, so I headed outdoors. As I walked those halls, every negative thing I could imagine began to flood my mind. I found a bench outdoors, sat down, closed my eyes, took a long, deep breath, and exhaled. I began to inhale slowly, counting to ten, then I exhaled for ten counts. As I kept breathing this way, I eventually found myself thinking of scriptures that speak of peace and thinking thoughts that are true, noble, right, pure, lovely, admirable, excellent, and praiseworthy.

Replacing the negative thoughts with intentional breathing helps to refocus your mind. The healing words of scripture are a bonus. Another benefit of having God's Word planted in your heart is your ability to use it to replace negative thinking.

This breathing technique turns your mind inward where the Holy Spirit resides inside of you, allowing Him to take over. It allows you to take captive those negative thoughts and make them obedient to Christ, which is what we're commanded to do in 2 Corinthians 10:5. It's as if you're breathing in His love, wisdom, grace, peace, and guidance, then exhaling His glory. Try that the next time a negative thought enters your mind.

5. Protect Your Personal Space

Living through a life trial can be an extremely heavy burden. Therefore, it is very important that you protect your personal space both physically and mentally by not allowing other people to dump on you when you're going through the storm. When the Bible says we are to carry each other's burdens (Galatians 6:2), that means we are to help one another in times of trouble.

You've heard the saying "misery loves company." Sometimes, when people see you going through a trial, they think it's appropriate to share all the drama in their lives in an effort to bond with you. This is NOT okay. Taking on additional, excessive burdens doesn't help you to endure your trial. You can be of no help to the person who seeks attention when you're in a dark place yourself.

I'm not saying that you shouldn't hear about anyone else's struggles at all, but I am warning you to watch for individuals who have a pattern of always complaining about life. During your trial, it may be best to limit or even discontinue the time spent with them to preserve your peace.

After my husband died, I allowed myself to get stuck in a situation that left me completely drained of all energy. After spending a good amount of time with an individual, I felt depressed after hearing so much complaining and negativity. And I decided that I needed to distance myself from that person for a time. I made no announcement about my intentions; it wasn't necessary. I simply did not make myself available to spend any more time with that person.

Please understand that it's okay to make yourself unavailable to anyone who brings negative energy when you're living through a life trial, or at any time, for that matter. It is very insensitive for a person to approach someone who they know is suffering a life storm to talk about how terrible their own lives are. I'm not saying you have to cut off friendships, but protect yourself by using discernment in who you allow into your space.

That being said, don't YOU be that person either. We all need someone to talk to when we're going through our trials. However, we need to be mindful of what we're saying and how much we're sharing with someone who's already suffering. Think about how your words may affect the listener. When I shared my journey on social media, my purpose was to glorify God. Although I was being transparent about my experiences, I never complained about my situation. And I made sure to always give praise to God while sharing. The Bible says:

"Do not let any unwholesome talk come out of your mouths, but only what is helpful for building others up according to their needs, so that it may benefit those who listen." (Ephesians 4:29)

Think about this while in the presence of others. Our words have potential to impact our listeners positively or negatively.

6. Live God's Word

Whatever you have planted in your heart is what you will draw from during a life trial. Reading the Bible, as we've discussed, is crucial. Attending church is an important part of growing in your faith. Participating in Bible studies is also helpful. But what's the purpose of gaining knowledge if you're not able to live it out? If your actions aren't guided by what you learn, what's it all for?

Do you remember what I shared earlier about the time I stepped down from all church ministries? Well, God has allowed me to see the fruit of that time spent with Him.

One day, while I was caring for my husband, I was exhausted and felt like I had no energy left in me. It was during a time when I was sleep deprived. On this particular day, I sat on the sofa, feeling completely defeated, and tears began to form in my eyes. I didn't want my husband to see me cry, so I went into the room next door. I kneeled beside the bed and started weeping quietly. I felt embarrassed to go before God because I had not been spending any time with Him that week. I said, "God, I'm so sorry. I know I haven't given you any of my time. I'm so tired. I'm tired, God. I have nothing left to give." My heart was torn because I really felt like I had let Him down, like He wasn't first in my life at that time.

I laid my head on the bed and allowed the tears to fall. Then, all of a sudden, I heard the heart of God in my spirit say, "My daughter, you are living my Word. You don't have anything to give, but I have everything to give, and it is through you that I will draw others to me. Keep living my Word."

Immediately, my mind flashed back to the day when I told God, "I know you are preparing me for something." I realized God had prepared me, all those years ago, for this day, for this season, for this trial. I started praising Him and thanking Him. I hugged myself and held on for a long time, crying and praising.

It is important to have God's Word planted in your heart, not for the sake of knowledge, but so that you can live it, in good times and in bad.

God says in His Word,

"Do not merely listen to the word, and so deceive yourselves. Do what it says. Anyone who listens to the word but does not do what it says is like someone who looks at his face in a mirror and, after looking at himself, goes away and immediately forgets what he looks like. But whoever looks intently into the perfect law that gives freedom, and continues in it—not forgetting what they have heard, but doing it—they will be blessed in what they do." (James 1:22–25)

As my Bible Doctrine instructor simply says, "Read the Book and do what it says."

7. Self-Care

I saved this final method of endurance for last because it includes a lot of important steps you should take to ensure your well-being. In fact, I believe it's so crucial that I decided to give the topic its own chapter. The amount of effort you put into taking care of yourself in the midst of a trial will reveal itself both physically and mentally—during and after the trial. So, let's take a look at four simple practices that will help to preserve your sanity and health during the storm.

Chapter 19

Self-Care

When my husband was ill and I was busy being a caregiver, people would tell me to make sure I was taking care of myself. I heard stories of caregivers dying before their patients from neglecting their own care. I wish I could tell you that self-care is easy when you're in the midst of a trial, but it's not. There were even times when I thought it was selfish to focus on self-care when my husband was suffering from cancer. But I knew that wasn't coming from a place of wisdom. I also knew that if I didn't take care of me, I wouldn't be able to take care of him. Neglecting your self-care while going through a trial will make matters worse, both during and after the storm.

I did what I could to stay healthy and keep my sanity. I've listed four tips below to help you take the necessary steps in taking care of yourself when faced with a life trial.

Rest

Sleep is golden. Without proper rest, you will not have enough energy to endure the difficulties and important matters that may present themselves during your trial. Being sleep deprived will also prevent you from addressing your other self-care needs. I know that many people are able to operate on a few hours of sleep and run on adrenaline, but after a while they crash—sometimes that even ends with hospitalization.

While I was caring for my husband, I suffered terribly at times from lack of sleep. Once his mental state became impaired, he didn't sleep much at night. He would bang on the headboard of his hospital bed throughout the night. Because I stayed on the sofa to be near him, I couldn't sleep either. And when he became bed bound, I needed to change his diapers, and I wanted him to be clean throughout the night.

At one point, I was so exhausted that I moved into the guest room a few feet away from his hospital bed, but I could still hear the banging. I felt like I was going to collapse from lack of rest.

One day I got the clever idea to pad the headboard with towels and tape. "Aha," I thought. "He won't be banging tonight." Wrong. He ripped the tape and towels right off and started banging again. All I could do was just lie down, cry, and pray for rest. There were times when my sons didn't have to work, and they would stay with him at night so I could sleep upstairs. Those were the best nights of sleep. I always woke up feeling totally refreshed and ready to take on the day.

Rest is imperative. Sleep deprivation feeds frustration, impairs judgment, causes extreme fatigue, breeds impatience, and heightens negative thoughts. Negative thoughts run wild when you're tired. Protect your sanity and health by getting as much rest as possible during a life trial.

Drink Water and Eat

Your body will respond to the way you treat it. It's very important to stay hydrated. If you're not drinking enough water daily, dehydration can send you to the emergency room, and that's the last thing you want when you're already dealing with a devastating life trial.

Eating a balanced diet is always important but even more so during a life trial. Your energy is being depleted at a more rapid rate due to the stresses you're undergoing, so if at all possible, eat as many fruits and vegetables as you can.

While I know how important it is to eat healthy, I also know that this is another area that is largely neglected during a crisis. Sometimes, eating anything at all is the last thing on your mind when you're suffering. The idea of having to prepare a meal is even more stressful, especially if you have a family to feed.

We were very fortunate to have a large community of friends who surrounded our family with love and support. They prepared and delivered many meals to us. But if that isn't something you can rely on, then you need to plan. In times like these, simplicity is the key. On days when I had to prepare meals, I kept it very simple and stuck with things that I could whip up quickly. My husband stayed hungry, all throughout his illness. He never lost his appetite during chemotherapy treatments, so I had to stay on top of his meals and snacks. I made sure to have things around that would satisfy his needs and mine at the same time. For example, he loved to eat crackers with peanut butter and slices of apple on top. That became my snack too.

Sticking with simple meals will reduce the stress of cooking. Also, cooking in large quantities and freezing meals for later will help tremendously.

Take Breaks

Everything that comes with living through a life trial can take a toll on your mental and physical health. For this reason, it's imperative to your well-being that you step away from the situation sometimes. Depending on your particular circumstance, it may be impossible to take a full day off. However, see if you can step away—if only for an hour—both mentally and physically. Maybe that will require someone else stepping into your place temporarily.

I was fortunate to have my sons or friends sit with my husband sometimes so that I could have a break. I treasured those moments of solitude. Once, a group of friends took me to the nail salon so that I could have a manicure and pedicure. Then, one day I went out to lunch at a local restaurant all by myself because I wanted to be alone.

I was part of a gourmet cooking club that met monthly for a potluck dinner. I had not attended the dinners while caring for my husband but decided one month that I wanted to go spend time with the ladies and get out of the house. I prepared my dish during the day while also tending to my other duties. When my oldest son returned home from work that evening, I went upstairs and got ready with a smile in my heart. I was so excited to be going out. I kissed my husband and son, grabbed my dish, sashayed out the door, and drove to the home of the hostess.

When I arrived, there were no cars parked outside and the exterior house lights were off. I thought maybe the other ladies were running late and the hostess just forgot to turn on the lights. I walked up to the house with my dish, rang the doorbell, and waited. As the hostess opened the door, I said, "Hi!" with a big smile. She looked at me with a question mark on her face and said, "Oh, hi, Anita!" I asked her where everyone was and if she was still having the dinner. She said, "Oh no! It's next week, Anita!" I had arrived at the dinner a whole week early! We both burst out with loud laughter. I hurried back to my car, drove home, and had myself a plate of whatever it was I made for the dinner. Although I didn't get to hang out with my friends, I did get a good belly laugh. Sometimes laughter is just as therapeutic as getting away.

I also started going back to the gym. I would get up early in the morning while my husband or sons were still asleep and drive to the gym while it was still dark outside. I would work out then head back home before the guys woke up. Starting my day with exercise had been my lifestyle for many years, and I really needed that release of adrenaline during that time. Unfortunately, it was short lived—after my husband started having seizures, I was afraid to leave him. So, I put my bike trainer next to his bed and used that for a while. If you have any way of exercising through your trial, take advantage of the opportunity to keep yourself active.

Perhaps you can't get away physically, but you can focus on something that makes your heart happy. Are you a reader? Do you paint? Is gardening the craft that brings you peace? Are you a musician, dancer, or poet? What can you do that takes you away mentally, to a place where peace resides?

Sewing is my happy place. A year and a half before my husband became ill, I launched a sewing blog and YouTube channel where I teach the basics of garment construction to those seeking to learn how to sew. I had no time or desire to sew while caring for him because I was too tired. But one day, I decided that I needed to sew for happiness. I moved my sewing machines to the kitchen table so I could watch my husband while I sewed. I started sewing pieces for myself and ended up with a mini collection of seven garments I could mix and match with each other. Then, when my husband went into the rehab hospital, I took my sewing machine with me a couple of times while I visited. I still can't believe I did that. I spent my days in the hospital with him and went home to sleep in the evenings. When I think back, those were the days when I remember feeling the most refreshed during our journey. I was sleeping at home, getting a full night of rest, and doing something that I loved.

Take time for yourself and do something that makes you smile, if only for thirty minutes to an hour. Maybe practice meditating on God's Word. Do whatever brings peace to your soul and use it to take a mental break from the situation.

Accept Help

Going through a trial in life can sometimes be lonely. If you don't have resources to tap into or people to walk alongside you in support, you may really feel like you're all alone. One of the most important things you can do for your life is to establish a support team of people who will do life with you, who will be there for you through good and bad. While God is always with us in times of trouble, He also created us to be in community with one another. And one of the benefits of community is carrying one another's burdens—being there for each other during tough times. The Bible says, "A friend loves at all times, and a brother is born for adversity" (Proverbs 17:17).

Now listen! If you're thinking, "I have a huge community of friends online," that's not what I'm talking about. Being connected virtually isn't the same as having real life friends, those you can see in person, people you can sit and spend time with. Social media has made it so much easier for us to isolate ourselves, neglecting one of our basic needs—in-person, human interaction. I'm not against social media at all. In fact, I'm a consumer and creator of social content. However, I believe that in-person relationships are exceedingly more beneficial. God brings people into our lives on purpose, and community is His gift to His people.

Because we had built relationships with people, both in person and virtually (on my end), our family was completely surrounded with support, love, and care during our trial.

Please hear this. You will never get to where God wants you to be on your own. You need other people, especially when you're living through a life trial. In the beginning of my husband's illness, I struggled terribly with asking for help. But I knew that our situation was way over my head, far beyond my ability to endure on my own.

Once I started asking for help and people responded with open arms, then I knew that it really was okay. But I didn't have to ask much because our community was coming to us, asking what we needed. Then there were those who didn't ask. They simply did whatever God placed on their hearts to do.

People want to help, and many will go out of their way to bless you in your time of need. God will use the people He has placed in your life to demonstrate His love. Right after I announced Cecil had a tumor, I asked for prayer, and my mind was blown over how many people joined us in prayer. I knew, then, that God was covering us. I saw the grace of God showing us how many people wanted to be there for us.

That was just the beginning of His abundant love being showered upon us through the people He had placed in our lives. They came from all over.

Coworkers

While my husband was in the ICU after his brain surgeries, a group of his fire brothers came by to visit. Before leaving, they asked me if there were any projects that we needed done around the house. To this day, I still can't believe what I said. All I could think about was blessing my husband. I whispered to them that he was planning to build a patio cover for our backyard. We didn't *need* a patio cover, but I asked because I knew it would make Cecil happy. I knew he would have never asked them to do that, and he told me later that he couldn't believe I asked for that.

Those men completely blew our minds. They formed crews of firemen who came to our home and built the most beautiful patio cover. They worked for weeks, on their days off work, in the blazing sun, day after day.

My husband kept saying, "I can't believe it." And there were times when he shed a few tears during the project because he saw the deep love they had for him. They kept showing up until that cover was complete.

At other times, fire brothers would drive out from far away just to do work around the house. They fixed things that were breaking, mowed our lawns, washed my car. I didn't need them to wash my car. I have two strong boys who could mow the lawns. But these were their ways of serving our family. They needed to be there for us in their own ways because their hearts loved Cecil. They wanted to be there for their brother, and I allowed them because it blessed their hearts to serve our family.

I had to humble myself each time someone asked if we needed anything. Receiving help is an act of humility, and because we've been conditioned to be independent, it can be difficult to let others in. Once I started to rest in the humility of receiving help, I realized that not only was I benefiting, but it was also a blessing to the givers. When you open yourself up to receiving their contributions in supporting you in your time of need, you will see just how much it helps them too. Our community wanted to be a part of our journey because they loved us. Not accepting help from people is a form of ungodly pride.

Church Members and Friends

Early on, our church set up a meal train for our family. Church members brought meals to us every day for a while. That blessed me more than I imagined it would. Cecil and I had been on the meal train for years, providing meals for other members of the church. But when we received the blessing of having others serve us in that way, I couldn't believe how helpful it was. Now, when I take a meal to a family, I totally understand how they feel to be on the receiving end. I stopped the meals after a while, but at one point my son accepted the invitation from the church to start it up again after Cecil started going back and forth to the hospital.

Eventually, I didn't need the church to bring meals and was doing fine on my own. But there were times when I had days that just didn't go as planned. One day I really needed to go to the grocery store, but it was one of those days—I just couldn't make it happen because things were off with my husband. All of a sudden, I received a call from a church friend saying she wanted to bring over some groceries. "WHAT?" I still get chills when I remember that moment. I was stunned and had to remember I was on the phone and needed to give this lady an answer. I told her how timely her offer was and that I would love to have the groceries.

There was another time when I was having a difficult day. It was almost time for dinner, and I had nothing prepared. At the very moment when I was wondering what I could make, I got a phone call from another church friend, asking if she and her husband could bring us food because they were at a restaurant and wanted to order something for us. I screamed—I mean literally screamed over the phone and told her what I was just going through. She said, "We're on the way." Another time, a couple drove to us from over two hours away to provide meals so I didn't have to worry about cooking. They delivered the meal, then got right back on the road to take that long drive back home.

Two different families provided Thanksgiving dinner for us in 2017. One of our fire families and our next-door neighbors thought of us. We literally had two full Thanksgiving meals. I was able to freeze food for later, which blessed my heart because I needed those meals for tough days when I couldn't do it.

This is what I mean when I say people will approach you in your time of need because they want to be there for you. They want to shower you with love. There are many more stories of my church family members reaching out to me and doing things that just took my breath away. There were boxes of groceries delivered to our home from Amazon. Several other people brought groceries to our home. Two friends allowed us to have their organic produce deliveries. The men would come help me get Cecil into the car so I could get him to doctor's appointments. Our pastor brought Communion to our home several times. I could probably write another book on their acts of kindness.

Secret Friends

When people show up to bless you from their hearts, in their own way, God always uses it not only to bless you but to teach you. I've learned some valuable lessons, but the private postcards taught me a lesson in humility. To this day I don't know who the sender was, but someone started sending me lovely postcards with beautiful handwritten notes while my husband was ill. The notes were so uplifting. I remember many times holding the cards to my chest after reading them, smiling, breathing in God's love, wondering who He was using to bless my heart so tenderly. Along with all the greeting cards we received over the course of our journey, I kept these postcards because of the impact they left on my heart. I still smile when I think of those cards.

The lesson I learned from the person who sent the cards is that we don't have to be seen to bless a person's heart. Giving in secret is a blessing that honors God.

People want to be there for you too. Allow them to bless you because in doing so you are receiving the love of God. Building relationships is important. Building community is important. Allowing people to serve you from their hearts with their gifts is important. When you find yourself in the midst of a trial, you're gonna need family and friends to walk alongside you. I can't tell you how comforting it is to have people supporting you in your time of need. If you think you can endure your trials without the help of others, please understand that it will be a very lonely journey. I can't imagine you being alone at a time when you truly need support. We need each other. We need community.

Support Groups

While having family and friends to support you during your trial is helpful, the reality is that after a while, they move on. And that's not to say they no longer support you or care, but they have their own lives too. There are times when you will need to seek help beyond your community. Some situations may require the services of professionals who are specifically equipped to deal with your particular situation. Therapy, counseling, rehabilitation, and support groups are just a few types of professional services you may want to consider to help you endure your specific trial.

After my husband's death, several people reached out to me and suggested I join a support group. At first I dismissed the suggestions because I thought I was doing a great job handling the grief. Then, one day a friend from church took me out to lunch and handed me a book called *Through a Season of Grief*, a devotional by Griefshare. She told me that she and her sister had gone through the book together after the death of her sister's husband. In the back of the book was the obituary of her sister's husband. My friend also made a custom bookmark for me with a beautiful message. My heart was really impacted by this for two reasons. First, I felt sorrow because another woman was experiencing the same pain that I was enduring. Second, two other people had mentioned that Griefshare offers support groups all over the country, and a man from the gym had invited me to a Griefshare group at his church.

I added the devotional to my morning Bible reading time. Not long after the lunch with my friend, someone asked me if I had considered joining a grief support group. For some reason, it clicked with me this time—perhaps God was sending these people to me because there was a need that I wasn't aware of. I think part of the reason I hesitated also was because my one and only encounter with a grief support group was when I accompanied my mother-in-law to a meeting after my father-in-law's death. It was very sad and somber. The last thing I wanted to do was sit in a room with a lot of people crying and looking sad.

Nevertheless, I logged onto the internet to find a Griefshare meeting near me. I invited my sons to go with me. Jordon declined, and although hesitant, Brandon agreed to accompany me to the first meeting.

We showed up, not knowing what to expect. When we walked inside, there was one large table with about ten or twelve people already seated. We grabbed our name tags and took a seat. The two facilitators introduced themselves and shared how the program worked. There was a round of introductions and the first class was underway. We watched a video, followed by discussion. Were there tears? Yes, but it wasn't the somber, sad environment that I had experienced before. This was different; we actually had lessons and workbooks to assist us in our discussions. I was very pleased with the format because I like direction and purpose.

I left that meeting with a smile on my heart. I had been in the company of people who understood what I was going through, to an extent, because they were grieving too. We shared with each other how we were coping with different parts of our grief. We shared our struggles and accomplishments. When the other guests shared things I was experiencing too, I felt relief. I realized that the things I was feeling and doing were a normal part of grieving. While my son didn't go back, I continued until the class ended and it was very beneficial for me.

As you can see, finding time to rest; nourishing your body with food and water; taking mental and physical breaks; and accepting help are four helpful ways to implement self-care during a life trial. While there are other things you can add to this list, be careful that you don't weigh yourself down by trying to do too much. Remember, rest is important so that you will be better prepared to do the hard things.

Chapter 20

Do Hard Things

No matter what type of trial you encounter in life, there will always come a time when you'll need to do hard things. There are no guidelines or instructions that teach you how to deal with the specific details associated with your storms. As life is happening, you either address the hard things or you don't. I can tell you this one thing for sure, from experience: dealing with the hard things will strengthen you for each step that you take thereafter. Running away, hiding, or ignoring the reality of your situation will only prolong the inevitable. At some point, you will have to deal with your hard thing.

After my husband died, I started receiving forms and documents in the mail concerning important matters that I needed to take care of in a timely manner. I was not in the state of mind, emotionally, to deal with these things, but I had to take care of business, no matter how I felt. If I hadn't addressed those issues, and put them off until I felt like it, it could have caused problems for me later. And because I'm the type who wants all things in order, I needed to tackle those tasks right away, for my own peace of mind. Therefore, I did what I had to do—some days with tears streaming down my face. There were times when I had to stop reading or filling out documents, for a moment, because the grief was so intense.

Doing hard things isn't simply a matter of doing what needs to be done. It's easy to look at your circumstances and say to yourself, "I'm gonna get through this. I will overcome it." I learned that doing hard things isn't just about getting them done; it was part of my healing, part of my growth. Healing and growth are painful at times, but through the pain you will achieve your greatest accomplishments in the season. Plus, I found that accomplishing the most dreaded hard things brought relief and liberation.

In dealing with forms and transferring things over from my husband's name to mine, I encountered situations that I never thought about. Things that I never considered until it was time to take that action. Changes that took my breath away. One such change happened the first time I visited the optometrist after Cecil's death.

My husband and I always went to the eye doctor together. When I showed up to my appointment alone for the first time, it felt kind of weird. I signed in and took a seat. As per routine, the receptionist called me over to take the clipboard and make any necessary changes since the last visit. Oh my goodness! I had forgotten all about that part. I sat down, looked at the forms and saw my husband's name listed as primary on insurance. Although I had already made the changes through our insurance carrier, I hadn't contacted the optometrist yet.

Immediately, my heart began to race, and I started taking deep breaths. Looking at the forms, I flashed back to times when we sat next to each other in that very space. I looked around at the tables where we used to put on our new contacts. I scanned the room, trying hard not to allow the tears to fall that were welling up in my eyes. As they began to trickle down, I scrambled to find a handkerchief in my purse. But I didn't grab it in time, and the tears began to fall onto the papers. Wiping my eyes first, then the papers with my handkerchief, I brought my attention back to the heartbreaking action I was about to take. I needed to remove my husband's name from the forms. Then I would request that they close out his file.

Remove him from the forms. Close his file. I couldn't really wrap my mind around what I had to do. In a strange way, it felt to me like he was dying again. How could I remove him? "Oh God, this is so cruel." I dabbed my eyes and began the task of making all the necessary changes. After I was done, I sat for a few minutes to work up the courage to walk over to the desk and tell the receptionist to close my husband's file. I finally did and asked if I could use the bathroom.

Walking the pathway to the bathroom, I felt unstable, like I would fall over at any moment. When I finally saw the door, I reached for the handle, rushed in, locked the door, and my emotions took complete control over my body. With one hand on the wall to hold myself up, and the other hand on my stomach, I buckled over in tears, crying quietly, the tears flowing heavily. The pain in my heart was agonizing. Turning my back towards the wall to keep from falling, I leaned on it, screaming quietly with both hands formed into fists pressed against the sides of my temples.

After moaning and crying for a few minutes, I washed myself up in the sink and went back into the waiting room. There weren't many people in the office at the time and I was glad—I didn't want anyone to see that I had been crying.

Shortly afterwards, my name was called, and I met the doctor at the desk. On the way to the examination room he said, "Where is the tall one?" He looked back at me and our eyes met.

"Cecil died," I said. He put both hands to his mouth and said, "Oh my God!" Then he grabbed and hugged me, saying, "Oh, I'm so sorry." Visibly shocked, he stood there with one hand on his chest. Then he walked me into the exam room. He sat down and put his hands to his head and asked what happened. I told him and he said he was sorry again. After talking for a bit, he did my exam, and I was done. I walked out of that office feeling sad but also liberated—I had done a hard thing. Could I have waited and done it at a later date? Of course I could have waited. However, dealing with it at that moment not only removed another task that I needed to complete but it also helped prepare me for the next change. I felt a bit courageous.

Putting off the inevitable doesn't necessarily make it easier. However, there are some things that are better left until later. Moving too quickly to deal with certain issues in the midst of your trial could also result in damage. The key is using discernment, and that comes from the Lord. Your emotions will ebb and flow during the trial, and learning to discern when to move or wait is crucial.

If you're feeling like you can take on the world one day and find yourself crying your eyes out the next, it's okay. There's nothing wrong with you. I would only caution you to be careful about the moves you make when you're living in the ebbs. Some decisions are a no-brainer, things you don't have to put any thought into. For instance, removing my husband as the primary on our insurance wasn't something I needed to think about. It was a necessary change for my sons and I to continue receiving medical services.

However, if you're in an emotional state and have to make a decision that isn't straight forward, waiting until you're in your flow would probably be best. After Cecil died, several people advised me, "Don't make any major decisions for the first year." I took that advice to heart, and I'm grateful. I wanted to do some things out of fear back then, but today I can say I'm glad that I didn't make those changes. Use discernment, and if you're not sure about which direction to take on an issue or are too emotional to address it (assuming it's not something that needs to be taken care of right away), give it time and go back to it later.

I had to do this very thing concerning my husband's clothes after he died. We shared a closet, and therefore I saw his clothing every day as I got dressed. In the beginning it was very sad to look over and see his clothes hanging there. They were a reminder of his absence, but after time they became a comfort for me. Some days I would walk over to his side of the closet and touch an item and tears would fill my eyes as I remembered him.

One day, while I was in the closet, I saw one of his robes and went to touch it. As I grabbed the sleeve and rubbed it gently across my right cheek, I bent over and sniffed the collar. Why did I do that? His scent was still on the robe, and I broke down crying. I pulled the robe from the hanger and held it to my nose, sniffing and sniffing, desperately wanting to take in more of his scent. Somehow I could feel him through the scent. I could hear his voice and see his face. I wanted more of him, so I sniffed harder and harder, not wanting to lose the scent. Moving my nose from one side of the collar to the next, searching for more of his scent, I sniffed and sobbed. My nose became clogged, then I couldn't smell anymore. Tears streaming down my face, I began to scream. "God! Oh, God! I want him back. God, please help me! Ohhh!" Groaning, as if in physical pain, holding tightly to the robe, I brought the robe to my chest, panting for air as I breathed through my mouth now. As my painful sobs filled the closet, I sat down on the floor and rocked back and forth, holding the robe to my chest. After a while, I began to calm down. I stood up, replaced the robe on the hanger, and left the closet.

Every time I went into the closet, the thought always entered my mind that "one day" I would need to remove his clothes. Two years passed before I would make that move. I tried a couple of times before but couldn't do it. When I say "tried," I mean I looked at the clothes and thought about it. But I couldn't bring myself to take the first step. Then one day I hired contractors to install tile flooring in a section of my home, including the closet. That meant I would have to remove everything from the closet, including his clothing, which I did. My plans were to replace them after the floors were completed because I wasn't ready to let them go. In a strange way, it felt like if I let his clothes go, it would be final. It felt like I would be erasing him from my life or getting rid of him. The thought of not seeing his clothes made me feel sad. I was holding onto a part of him in my mind.

After the tile work was done, I put everything back where it belonged, except my husband's clothing. I intentionally left them in the guest closet. Shortly afterwards, I started a huge decluttering project, which included a virtual yard sale. This was during the 2020 pandemic, so I created an online sale for my friends to come over and get what they wanted while being socially distant.

One day, my best friend, Tina, and her husband, Bill, came to pick up some of the items. While they were on the way, the thought entered my mind that it was time to let the clothes go. The timing was divine because Bill is the only person I had ever considered giving Cecil's clothing to. My husband adored Bill and they were the same height and size. So I called Tina and told her I wanted Bill to take a look at Cecil's clothing when they arrived to see if he wanted to take them.

When they walked into the house, Bill saw the clothes and started trying things on. The smile on his face melted my heart. He was so happy and grateful. He loved Cecil's clothes and took everything I was giving away. Brandon and I watched him as he tried on the clothes. After they left, Brandon told me that he had to turn away to keep from crying when Bill tried on Cecil's favorite green button-down shirt.

When Bill tried on a couple of the jackets, I became a little emotional, but I kept myself together. Bill and Tina gathered the clothing and other items, loaded them into the car as we laughed and chatted, then drove away. After they left, I went into the house and cried my eyes out. I felt sad that his clothes were gone. But I was also grateful because his clothes went to someone who I knew would cherish them, someone Cecil loved.

I didn't realize it at the time, but I had taken a step that would help move me forward in my healing journey. Doing the hard thing released me from the burden of always thinking about "one day."

When you are in the midst of a trial and come face to face with decisions and actions that seem beyond what your heart can bear, do the hard thing. Doing hard things in the midst of your trial opens the way to clarity about next steps. It clears the path for you to move forward. Doing one hard thing leads to the next step, then the next. Eventually, when another hard thing presents itself, you will have built up a storage of courage.

Here's one last story to demonstrate how a storage of courage will serve you when needed. Think of the storage as a memory bank. With each act of perseverance through hard things, you're depositing memories of how you've worked through difficult decisions or actions. When you're faced with the next difficult task, make a withdrawal from your storage of courage as a reminder, and do the hard thing. It's liberating to walk away from something you first dreaded with a sense of accomplishment.

I was fortunate to experience this feeling of liberation about one year after my husband's death. Up until that point, I had avoided the hospital where Cecil was treated and where we'd eventually received his hospice recommendation from. But I knew that one day I would have to go back. It was inevitable.

That day came in January 2020, the day I was scheduled to board a plane heading to Memphis, Tennessee, to celebrate my grandmother's 100th birthday. My dear friend's daughter texted me to say that her mom had suffered a stroke and was in the hospital. I was in the parking lot at a convenience store, about to head to the freeway.

Shocked by the news, I turned off my car and asked which hospital her mom was in and if she was receiving visitors. She gave me the information and confirmed that my friend could have visitors. After hanging up the phone, I sat there for a few minutes, dreading the idea of walking into that hospital.

I tried to get out of it by telling myself that I really needed to get on the freeway and head out of town. I told myself that I could check on her while I was away and visit her at home when I returned from my trip. But those were excuses to avoid the hospital.

Then I thought about my friend and felt embarrassed for even considering not going to see her. This was not about me. I remembered how good it made me feel when people showed up for my husband when he was ill. I remembered how unselfish people were in being there for us. Who was I to not be there for my friend? How dare I not show up?

I started the car and rushed over to the hospital. As I pulled into the parking lot, I took in a deep breath and exhaled slowly. I did that over and over. Driving past the front entrance, I looked over in that direction and quickly turned my head back forward. "Oh gosh! Oh my gosh! Whew! God, help me to do this." More deep breaths. I found a parking spot, turned off the car, and just sat there shaking my head. I took a few more deep breaths, opened the car door, stepped out, and began walking toward the entrance.

As I prayed my way to the door and entered, I felt like my heart would explode. I could literally feel my heart pounding as I continued down the hallway to the check-in desk. After receiving the visitor's sticker, I entered the elevator and pressed the button to the floor that my husband had been admitted to several times. On the quick ride up, I prayed, "God, please don't let this be the same room he was in. Please don't let me see any of the staff who cared for him. Don't let me see the doctor who said 'hospice.'"

"Ding!" The elevator doors opened, I stepped out, made a right turn, then a left. I began walking the long hallway—and who did I see first? The physical therapist that took him walking down the halls during his visits before he lost all mobility. It was the kind young man who gave us his own fingertip blood pressure monitor to take home because he just wanted us to have it. He really respected my husband because of his job and always showed up to the room with a great smile on his face and handled Cecil so gently.

When I saw him, I gasped quietly and said, "Oh my gosh! Oh, God!" Taking deep breaths, I picked up my pace, made a quick left turn and began heading down another hallway. Then I saw it, the nurses' station.

"Oh no! Oh, God, please don't let me see them," I whispered as I slowed my pace almost to a halt.

Then I started talking to myself. "Get yourself down that hallway. You can do this! You've got this! She needs your support. Hold your head up! Get to that room!" I picked up my pace again, held my head high, began to swing my arms, walking with intention now. As I passed the nurses' station I glanced over to the right and thought I saw the nurse who was in the room with me when he was placed on hospice. I took a deep breath and kept walking. At the end of the hallway, I made a right turn and started looking at the room numbers. I passed by one room that he had stayed in and prayed again that she wouldn't be in one he visited. I spotted the room and took a huge sigh of relief. He hadn't been in that room, so I stepped in and said, "Hello?" My friend and her husband turned to see me, and she was so surprised. I could tell she was delighted. I visited for a while, prayed with her, and left. On the way out, I didn't worry about who I would see. I kept my head up, and once I rounded that last corner leading to the elevator, I even began to smile.

I couldn't believe how good I felt. There was a sense of accomplishment as I exited the hospital and walked through the parking lot. When I sat down in my car, I put my hands on my chest, bent over, and said, "Oh my goodness! Thank you so much, God! Oh, God! I did it! I did it!" I started the car and drove away with a great sense of pride—I did the hard thing.

Listen, your hard thing is specific to your situation. What may be hard for you could be a piece of cake for the next person. Visiting a hospital where a loved one stayed many times before dying may not be a big deal at all for someone else. But for me, it was huge. And you know what happened? Every time I drove past the hospital after that visit, I never thought, "God, I never want to go there again," like I had before visiting my friend.

Doing the hard thing will give you clarity and peace of mind. It releases you from the burden of dread. It boosts your confidence for future hard things. And finally, you walk away with a sense of accomplishment.

Just as standing in your faith and trusting the sovereignty of God are foundational elements to stepping into purpose during a life trial, enduring the trial with grace is crucial to your future well-being. All three steps, working together, are pivotal in moving you into the fourth. If you are seeking to please God along this journey of stepping into His purpose, you must proceed into His calling.

Part 5

PROCEED

"Now get up and stand on your feet.
I have appeared to you to appoint you
as a servant and as a witness of what
you have seen and will see of me."

(Acts 26:16)

Chapter 21

God's Invitation

To reach a destination, a person must be actively engaged in taking steps that lead to that location. God has designed a path that is unique to the person He created you to be. While proceeding along the path, you will encounter bumps in the road, obstacles to overcome, and hills to climb. Remember, God never promised you an easy, trouble-free life. So, when you come face to face with a trial, just remember that the One who created you has gone before you. He's paved the way for you to overcome and proceed to the destination He has ordained for your life—obedience to His call.

Proceeding, in this case, is a continuation of a course of action that has already begun. When God created you, He designed you with intention to carry out His plans of advancing His kingdom. You are His ambassador, a vessel by which others will be drawn to Him. The way this plays out on your end will manifest itself based on what you believe. Our beliefs are our mindsets, based on our experiences in life. Some mindsets serve us well as we seek to honor God with our obedience. Other mindsets completely sabotage us, paralyzing us and preventing us from believing we can answer His call to obedience.

For many of us, these mindsets were developed in childhood as we encountered experiences and practices handed down from our parents and others in our lives. For others the negative mindsets were learned later in life through abusive relationships and other experiences. Unless we learn to change our own narratives, we'll continue to carry these negative mindsets with us throughout life and never fully step into the obedience of who we were created to be.

Mindsets from Childhood Memories

For many years of my life, I sought perfection as a way to fit in—I thought I needed to prove myself worthy. This was a subconscious desire, and I didn't realize I was doing this to myself at the time. But later I came to understand the "why" behind my thinking. A few childhood memories gave me clarity about my need to feel validated by people.

Growing up, I lived with my mother and sisters. My father was around sometimes, but I don't have memories of him being a strong figure or positive influence in my life. However, I do remember how happy I was to see him whenever he came home after being incarcerated and away from our family for long periods of time.

When I was a little girl, an incident with my father contributed to my later years of feeling like I was unworthy. It made such an impact on me that I still remember it vividly to this day.

He had been gone for a long time, and I don't remember if he was in jail or just gone away from our family. My sister and I were little girls, playing on the floor in a bedroom next to the living room. All of a sudden, the front door opened, and my father walked into the house with his friend trailing behind. As soon as we heard his voice, my sister and I jumped up and ran to him, screaming with excitement. We were so loud that he and his friend became startled and they both jumped. My father didn't stop to hug us or pick us up. He just kept walking. I don't remember what happened later. Maybe he did engage with us, but I only remember the sad feeling I had because we scared him. It felt as if scaring him cancelled out any joy he would have had upon seeing our faces. I felt sad that seeing us didn't elicit the same excitement from him that my sister and I expressed upon hearing his voice. I also remember wishing we had not scared him so that he would have been happy to see us. While it may seem insignificant, that incident made a huge impact on my thinking. I internalized it to mean that I wasn't important to him. This became part of my mindset—"I'm not important enough."

Another childhood incident that impacted me occurred when I showed up at a neighborhood kid's party. The kids on our block all played outside together where I grew up. We went from yard to yard and played in the streets during the day, and everyone was back to their homes when the streetlights came on. One kid didn't play outside with us all the time—his family kept him kind of sheltered. They didn't really like our family and were probably trying to protect him from us because there was trouble at our home sometimes.

On this particular day, this child was having a birthday party and the neighborhood kids were sitting outside on the steps of his home. I joined the kids and took a seat. We were giggling and laughing, waiting for the party to start. Then I looked back and saw his mom and another lady pointing at me from the front door. Immediately, I felt singled out because I had not been invited to the party. But we didn't do party invitations back then. If there was a party on the block, all the kids went. But when I saw them pointing, I knew they were talking about me not belonging there. I felt horrible and embarrassed. I wanted to stay with all the other kids, but I knew those adults didn't want me there. I don't remember if I stayed at that party, but I do remember how uncomfortable I felt that they were pointing at me. Again, I internalized this as part of my mindset—"I'm not invited. I don't belong."

The last childhood occurrence that impacted my mindset came from the idea that kids were to be seen and not heard, a popular teaching in the era in which I grew up. If you were in a room with adults and they were talking, you stayed quiet. The adults were seeking to teach us to respect our elders. I learned to respect adults, but I also subconsciously internalized it negatively. It became yet another negative piece I added to my mindset—"What I have to say isn't important. I don't have a voice."

Many of us never come to realize that the negative messages we've internalized from our past have shaped our current thinking and subsequent actions in life. Even worse, if we never change our narratives, we pass the same teachings down to our own children, in turn, creating cycles of bondage, limiting beliefs, low self-esteem, and lack of confidence. When I look back on these three occurrences from my childhood, what I gathered about myself was this:

"You're not important enough to be invited in life because nobody wants to hear what you have to say."

Nobody intentionally set out to teach me this way of thinking. In fact, my mother always told us that we were loved, important, and capable of achieving our goals. She instilled decent morals in her girls. We were taught to be kind to others and never to think we were better than the next person. She was adamant that we never call another person ugly and always made us hug each other after a fight. (I still don't agree with that hugging thing, though—I hated that.) Yet, with all the good things that she taught us, which I still live by to this day, I managed to embrace a negative mindset through my experiences.

But here's the thing—most people would never know that. I didn't even know it myself for a long time. I thought I was the bomb, in a secret kind of way. I never went around bragging about myself, but I knew how to conduct myself with dignity and grace, how to look the part, and how to show up. As far as I knew, I was living life well. I had a level of confidence about myself that allowed me to excel in most of the things I set out to do and make great accomplishments. Yet there was always a bit of insecurity lurking in the background.

We all take away from our experiences lessons that teach us, lessons that can help us to grow, and lessons that can discourage and paralyze us. What we do with the discouraging and paralyzing lessons is up to us. We can choose to embrace them, pass them on to others, or become transformed through the reconditioning of our minds.

"Do not conform to the pattern of this world, but be transformed by the renewing of your mind. Then you will be able to test and approve what God's will is—his good, pleasing and perfect will" (Romans 12:2).

Embracing New Mindsets

Over the years, I've learned how to shift my negative mindset to one more beneficial to God's purpose. The renewing of my mind has come through learning about Him and choosing to believe what He says about me. But here's the thing: shifting from a negative mindset isn't something that happens overnight. When you have lived most of your life not believing—or even knowing—who you were created to be, it takes time to make the shift. And once you change your way of thinking, there will still be times when you come face to face with a crisis of belief.

When this happens, you have a choice to make. You can believe the negative thoughts and never move forward into obedience. Or you can acknowledge them for what they are—lies—and allow the new narrative you've written for yourself to take center stage. Limiting beliefs can creep back in, even after you've written a new narrative. In fact, this happened during my book-writing journey.

On February 28, 2020, I got into my car and drove to San Diego to attend the Authors Who Lead Writers' Workshop. I arrived safely, checked into the hotel, and turned in early so that I would be well rested for the workshop the next day. I felt empowered, like I could do anything.

The next morning, I woke up refreshed and ready for a new adventure. But as the time neared for me to leave, I began to feel nervous. What in the world had I gotten myself into? I had no idea what to expect, but there was no turning back. I drove to the venue, parked my car, took a deep breath, got out, and walked over to the building. I entered the room like I was ready. I was excited to meet other people who were there to get educated about writing their first books too.

I was a little early and the organizers greeted me with such grace that I immediately felt relaxed. I found a seat at a table, center front, and put my items there to save the spot. Other guests started arriving and we mingled with each other until we were called to take our seats.

The first activity was an introduction. We had to state our names, how many books we had written, our nickname growing up, and how it came to be. The sound of screeching tires reverberated through my brain. "Wait! What? Time out! What was he talking about? How many books have we written? Weren't we all beginners?" I would soon find out that was not the case.

The introductions began to the far-right side of the room. As each person introduced themselves, my heart began to beat a little faster. These people were already authors. They were doctors, business owners, very established professionals from different industries. "Oh my gosh," I thought. "What am I doing here? I don't belong here." (You see how the negative mindset showed up again?) They had already written books, lots of books. One guy at my table had published *ten* books. A lady at another table had published about *fifteen* books. The man sitting next to me had already written and published his first book. The lady sitting to my right with her son had already written her first book and was about to publish. "God, what's happening? What are you doing?" I questioned in my heart.

As the introductions continued and my turn grew closer, I wanted to crawl under the table. If only there was a way I could exit the room without anyone noticing. I wanted to make a mad dash for the door, but I began to talk to God silently instead. "God, I don't know why you have me in the room with this group of people, but I trust you. I don't have a fraction of the experience that is present in this place, but I have you. And I know that you do all things with intention, purpose, and excellence. You brought me here, so I belong. I belong here. Have your way, oh God. Show me. I belong here." My heart began to settle as I embraced the truth by changing my thoughts.

When it was my turn, I introduced myself and stated that I was there to learn how to write my first book. It was the simple truth from my heart. All I had to offer was myself and a desire to learn, and that was enough for God. I had to crush the negative thoughts and trust Him. He showed me that I was there by His assignment so that I would see what He could do. I needed to be in the room with those who were already in the space where God was leading me. It was for my benefit to see them face to face, to listen to their language, to talk with them and see that they were normal everyday people, just like me. God allowed me to attend that event to meet my book coach in person, so that he could start me on my book-writing journey—something I never imagined I would ever do.

I went into this assignment knowing that I was supposed to share the message to encourage you and others as you walk through your own trials. But God used this assignment to help me first. I needed to continue my healing through the journey of writing the book. I needed to get deep with my past. I needed to shed tears over the memories. I needed to step into the pain of my past experiences and realize that they don't define me. They don't define me. THEY DON'T DEFINE ME!

Before I could encourage you or anyone else in this space, first I had to do the work. I had to come with my own experience. If I were to give you advice about persevering through trials, never having gone through the steps that I recommend myself, you probably wouldn't want to hear from me. Embracing a new mindset for yourself produces an awakening to who you are in Christ. Your identity in Christ has always been a part of you but has been overshadowed by the negative mindsets you've embraced over time. Maybe it hasn't felt powerful enough to manifest itself fully because of the lies you have believed about yourself. God wants to strip away the negative mindsets you've formed and replace them with His truth. He wants to use you wherever you are, whether it be in the midst of a storm or in the aftermath of devastation. God can and will use your trial as a catalyst by which you will be fully awakened to His call. And here's the reality: the call will oftentimes scare you. It's okay. Do it anyway. Do it scared.

Do It Scared

When God shows you what He wants you to do and starts prompting your heart, get ready. He will provide opportunities, open doors, and send people to confirm His assignment. Your job is to step into it.

When you become aware of what God is calling you to do through the awakening, your first reaction may be fear. You may be afraid that you're not experienced enough to carry out the assignment. You may wonder if you're hearing correctly. You may even think that it's something you've made up on your own, that it can't possibly be from God. These are all natural reactions when the mind has been conditioned to living in the comfort zone.

There's nothing comfortable about stepping into God's calling. Most often it requires embarking on new territory. Sometimes He will call you to an assignment that seems utterly impossible. Other times He calls you to something that may not be huge but is nevertheless scary. For example: if you're an introvert, perhaps He's calling you to open up more and interact with people. That may be a very scary and uncomfortable task for an extreme introvert. Perhaps you're new to the faith and He's calling you to start a Bible Study. That can be very intimidating to someone who doesn't know much about the Bible. Maybe you have overcome great obstacles in life and He's calling you to get on stages and speak to thousands of people about your experiences. If public speaking is a huge fear for you, then stepping onto a stage to speak may seem like an impossible task.

Whatever God calls you to do that evokes fear in your heart, do it scared. Don't wait until you feel confident. You can spend days, weeks, months, even years preparing for the day when you'll feel ready to answer the call. Newsflash! That day never comes. The only way to walk in obedience to God's call is to just step into it. Now.

I was invited to speak at a women's retreat for my church, ten months after my husband's death. That seemed exceedingly far beyond my ability at the time; I was still very deep in my grief. I knew the biannual retreat was coming up, but before receiving the invitation, I wasn't planning to attend.

As I was leaving church one day, the Retreat team was handing out flyers for the event. I took the flyer and placed it inside my Bible. When I got home, I placed the flyer on the end table, along with a stack of other papers. One day I was going through the papers and came across the flyer. Although I had no plans of attending the retreat, I decided to read the information anyway.

The first thing I noticed was that it was being held at a hotel near the beach in Ventura, California. I gasped, then squealed. Then I said to myself, "Oh, I'm going to Retreat!" In previous years, our church had held their retreats at campground-type venues. While the events were fine, I'm just not the camping type. I don't like rooming with a lot of people in bunkbeds. It's just not my thing. So when I saw that the retreat was to be held at a hotel, I was all in. I continued reading to get all the information and find out when registration would open.

The next thing I noticed was that there was no speaker listed on the flyer. In past years, they had always secured a speaker before printing flyers for the event. The first thought that came to my mind after seeing the speaker vacancy frightened me: "You're the speaker." I remember thinking to myself, "Oh my gosh!" I couldn't understand why I had that thought, and it felt very uncomfortable.

As I continued reading, I remember thinking afterwards, "Why would I think that? That will never happen!" I put the flyer aside and continued looking through the other papers, still a bit disturbed over my thought. I didn't make reservations for Retreat right away but planned to do it later.

One day I showed up at church early and took my seat, which was unusual for me. Returning to church after Cecil's death, I was always late. I don't even know why, but I always managed to walk in after praise and worship was in full swing. As I waited for service to start, the Women's Ministry Leader came over and we greeted each other. She began to tell me that the Retreat team was in discussions about a speaker for the following year and my name kept coming up.

I think my heart stopped beating at that point. I know she kept talking but I don't remember anything else she said after "your name." I flashed back immediately to that day I was reading the flyer and heard, "You're the speaker." I think I stared at her in disbelief for a couple of seconds, because she asked me to pray about it and let her know. I said okay, took my seat, and she walked away.

My heart was pounding out of my chest at this point. I didn't know what to do with my hands. I was in shock. After about thirty seconds, I said to myself, "Pray for what? I don't have to pray. The Holy Spirit has already revealed to me that I'm the speaker." I stood up, turned around, and spotted the Women's Ministry Leader in back of the church. I walked over to her and said, "I'm gonna say yes right now before I talk myself out of it." She smiled and I walked back to my seat, trembling all over.

I need you to understand that when I said yes to that assignment from God, I didn't know how I was going to do it. But because I got a clear call from God, I chose to obey.

The retreat was nine months away, so I decided not to do any preparing right away. Instead, I wanted to allow God to reveal what He wanted me to share as I continued to heal. And what I quickly learned was that He had already been writing the message on my heart throughout the journey. He had already been equipping me to stand before the women He had ordained to be in the room that weekend. So for nine months, I listened, watched, and waited. I listened to God speak healing into my heart. I watched Him reveal more and more of Himself. And I waited for

Him to do through me that which I agreed to do for Him. When the time was right, I began writing the message.

During preparation for the Retreat, God gave me scriptures to hold onto, scriptures to remind me that He had indeed chosen me and was with me. I want you to capture these verses in your heart. These are powerful words that will uplift and encourage you when you find yourself face to face with an assignment from God that you don't believe you're capable of accomplishing. This is what you need to remember when you set out to serve Him in excellence.

The following scriptures are His promises to you when He calls you into your next assignment. He says:

"I will instruct you and teach you in the way you should go; I will counsel you with my loving eye on you." (Psalm 32:8)

"I have chosen you and have not rejected you. So do not fear, for I am with you; do not be dismayed, for I am your God. I will strengthen you and help you; I will uphold you with my righteous right hand." (Isaiah 41:9–10)

"Commit to the Lord whatever you do, and he will establish your plans." (Proverbs 16:3)

"Peace be with you! As the Father has sent me, I am sending you." (John 20:21)

"Now get up and stand on your feet. I have appeared to appoint you as a servant and as a witness, of what you have seen and will see of me." (Acts 26:16)

For me, public speaking has always been one of the most terrifying things in the world. Although I had spoken publicly several times before the retreat, just the thought of standing before those women made my heart beat terribly fast. I was afraid, and all the limiting beliefs came like a flood.

When God calls you to do something that you feel is beyond your ability and it frightens you, do it scared. He will be with you—and you are in the most amazing company with God. As you step into obedience,

He comforts you with His powerful presence and strengthens you with His Word.

On the evening that I was to take the stage for the first speaking session at the retreat, I stood behind a closed door, waiting to hear my cue to walk out. I told the coordinator that I didn't want to engage with anyone beforehand because I would be totally zoned out. When I heard my name announced, the last thing I remember saying was, "Help me, Jesus."

I walked out to a full room of about ninety women, all standing and applauding. As I stood there, taking it all in, I felt the presence of God with me. It was as if He had ushered me onto the stage and said, "I have chosen you. Go and encourage my daughters." I looked around at their faces, then I went through the room and hugged as many of them as I could. I already knew these women, but I needed to connect with them through touch in that moment and God used it to settle my heart. When I made it back to the stage, I opened my mouth and spoke what God had placed on my heart. Through five speaking sessions over the weekend, God allowed me to share my story and encourage His daughters. Was I perfect? Absolutely not. Did I mess up at times? Sure did. Did the audience care? Not at all.

The only thing that mattered for me that weekend was being obedient to what God had called me to do. He had written the message on my heart and those who needed to hear it received what God had intended.

However, obedience to God's call usually doesn't come without a spiritual battle. If you've been delivered from the bondage of a negative mindset, be watchful that you don't revert back to your limiting beliefs. If you're not careful, you will fall victim to Satan's agenda.

Chapter 22

Combating Satan's Agenda

When you begin to change the narrative of a negative mindset, become fully awakened to God's call, and step into it, you will eventually come face to face with the enemy, Satan, the devil. Remember, the enemy's job is to prevent you from anything that brings honor and glory to God.

Satan's Agenda

When it comes to stepping into God's call on your life, the enemy's goal is to evoke fear in your heart, to shut you down, to prevent the light of God from shining through, and to paralyze you from moving forward. He will devise lies and accusations that sound an awful lot like your negative mindsets. Your ability to persevere through these tactics will be largely dependent upon the new narrative you've written for yourself and that which you have planted in your heart.

Maybe you are living through a trial right now and hearing the promptings from God, an invitation to join Him, a call that requires you to step into something unfamiliar, something scary. What thoughts keep you from moving forward?

Perhaps you've overcome a past trial and have moved forward with your life but know deep in your heart that you ignored the promptings from God to step into His call in that season. What thoughts kept you from obedience?

We learn from the Bible that the enemy is constantly on the prowl for victims, looking for an opportunity to devour the child of God (1 Peter 5:8). Satan knows how to use your negative mindsets and limiting beliefs to his advantage. What limiting beliefs do you have? Do you recognize them?

Imposter Syndrome

We can't have a discussion about stepping into God's calling and getting rid of limiting beliefs without mentioning these two little words that have the potential to shut it ALL down. Many refer to it as the inner voice that tells you negative things about yourself. But I call it an outer voice, because the voice of the Holy Spirit is the only one that has permission to reside inside of me. It's the voice of the adversary that says you're not good enough, not smart enough, not pretty enough, not anything enough. It wants to render you ineffective in your worship and service to God. It's called imposter syndrome. I had never even heard of such a thing until I was preparing to speak and stumbled upon a video about it.

After I said yes to speaking at the retreat, that imposter syndrome tried to wear me out. Here are the limiting beliefs I heard.

Who do you think you are?

I thought about the women who had spoken at Retreat in past years and believed they were way out of my league. So how could little old me speak at a retreat for an entire weekend?

You're not a speaker!

I didn't feel qualified to stand before these women to share about the power of God.

Nobody wants to hear from you!

I wondered if it was only the Retreat team who was interested in having me speak, and if the other women would think it was a bad idea.

You have a limited vocabulary!

I had heard other speakers deliver their talks with great intelligence, using words that were not part of my vocabulary.

You're gonna make a fool of yourself!

I kept thinking, "What if I get on stage and forget what I was gonna say? Do I really know what I'm talking about? What if it's a big old flop and nobody likes it?"

You sin every day, so you're a fake!

This was the worst because I had to deal with it daily. I kept thinking, "I don't measure up to God's standards. I mess up every day. They're gonna see right through me and know that I'm not qualified to stand on that stage."

I remember going back and forth with these thoughts one day. Then I found myself thinking, "Well, it really is true. I'm not really a speaker because I say I'm not. I don't have an extensive vocabulary. And I do sin every day. I guess this is my truth." But here's the reality. If my truth isn't aligned with God's truth, then my truth is a lie. I had to stop believing the enemy's voice. I would not allow the father of lies to infect my spirit and keep me in a space of mediocrity and safety.

My comfort zone of playing small and not fully stepping into who God created me to be was easy. You see, I was good at what I did—as I worked within the confines of my abilities, what I thought I was capable of accomplishing on my own. But when called to go higher, to reach farther, to tread unknown territory, I always questioned.

All the thoughts and beliefs that I mentioned above have the potential to prevent you from stepping into His call and proceeding along the path He's designed for you. Maybe you have a list of your own. As you seek to rewrite your own narrative, one of the most important things you can do is to identify what negative mindsets and limiting beliefs keep you from moving forward in obedience to God's call.

If that means writing them down on a sheet of paper or notebook, take the time to do that and follow my lead in the next section to combat those thoughts. It's time to pull out God's combat ammunition.

"Now get up and stand on your feet. I have appeared to you to appoint you as a servant and as a witness of what you have seen and will see of me." (Acts 26:16)

Combat Ammunition

We learn in the Bible that Jesus was tempted by Satan in the desert for forty days and nights. Jesus used scripture to combat the wickedness of the enemy's attempt to twist God's Word to fit his agenda. Every time Satan tried to benefit by using scripture, Jesus responded by saying, "It is written . . ." Because Jesus is our example, we too can use scripture to speak God's truth when the adversary attacks our identity and tries to distract us with lies and accusations about God's calling. The Bible says to put on the full armor of God so that you can take your stand against the devil's schemes. The Bible is described as the sword of the Spirit among the six armor pieces (Ephesians 6:10–18). Use this sword of the Spirit— the Bible—as your ammunition against the enemy.

God's Word Is Ammunition

Yet again, God's Word, planted in your heart, will come to serve you. When imposter syndrome is in full effect, the Word of God will be your weapon. Here is how I replied to the lies and accusations when the enemy tried to distract me from God's call.

1. When the enemy said, "Who do you think you are?" It is written:

"You are a chosen people, a royal priesthood, a holy nation, God's special possession, that you may declare the praises of him who called you out of darkness into his wonderful light." (1 Peter 2:9)

Believe who God says you are in His Word. There are countless verses in the Bible that speak of your identity in Christ (see Chapter 19). Use your weapon against the enemy.

2. When the enemy said, "You're not a speaker!" It is written:

"I can do all this through him who gives me strength." (Philippians 4:13)

Your beliefs about what you can do are usually based on your knowledge and skills. What God calls you to do will sometimes defy all reason. It will not make sense at times. When you are walking in the Spirit, no call of God is too big for you.

3. When the enemy said, "Nobody wants to hear from you!" It is written:

"You must go to everyone I send you to and say whatever I command you. Do not be afraid of them, for I am with you." (Jeremiah 1:7–8)

God has surrounded you with people who need to experience the calling He has placed on your life. Through your gifts and talents, He will draw them unto Himself. Then He will multiply the blessings by using them to further spread the calling. Go wherever He sends you with the authority you've been given, because He goes with you.

4. When the enemy said, "You're not wise enough! Speakers are smart!" It is written:

"If any of you lacks wisdom, you should ask God, who gives generously to all without finding fault, and it will be given to you." (James 1:5)

God is always available to guide you along the path He's designed for you. When you seek His direction with all your heart, He will show you the way. If there is anything you don't know, pray and ask God. He opens doors and provides wisdom for those who seek Him. When He calls you to an assignment, He wants your heart—not someone else's education.

5. When the enemy said, "You're gonna make a fool of yourself!" It is written:

"But God chose the foolish things of the world to shame the wise." (1 Corinthians 1:27)

Be the fool. They who the world sees as foolish, God rewards with wisdom and growth—provided they walk in obedience.

6. When the enemy said, "You sin every day, so you're a fake." It is written:

"All have sinned and fall short of the glory of God, and all are justified freely by his grace through the redemption that came by Christ Jesus." (Romans 3:23–24)

Once you have repented and stepped into obedience, your past sins have no power over your present and future. Rather, your forgiven sins are a testimony to the power of God to change you and use you for His glory. God doesn't seek perfect people. Your obedience to Christ is part of your transformation. You will never be free of sin until you are home with God.

The enemy will bully you and try to talk you out of doing what God tells you to do, but remember:

"The word of God is living and active. Sharper than any double-edged sword, it penetrates even to dividing soul and spirit, joints and marrow; it judges the thoughts and attitudes of the heart." (Hebrews 4:12)

Use the Word of God to combat the lies and accusations. Remember who you are in Christ. God will walk you through anything that He calls you to do, and He will never put you out there alone.

One day, as I was preparing to speak at the Women's Retreat in 2019, I suddenly felt like I couldn't do it. I had already completed writing the message and was planning to organize everything and time the sessions. I started with Friday's session, and before I could get halfway through, the timer went off.

I had no concept of how much written content would fill a particular time frame. I remember thinking, "What have I done?"

I started crying and asking God, "Why? God, why do I have to do this? I don't want to speak at this retreat. It's too much. It's too heavy, too much responsibility. I need my husband. He was always here to support me. You can't use me in this condition, God. I'm too weak. I've got too much healing to do. I don't want to do this."

I sat curled up in the chair beside my bed, next to the window, tears running down my face. I started to wonder how I could get out of speaking. What could I say to make them understand that I'm not cut out for this right now? The feeling of intense overwhelm weighed so heavily upon me as I sat there, crying and dreading the day I said yes to that assignment.

"God, what am I gonna do?" I asked. "Please help me." I sat there in silence for a while, listening, when all of a sudden, I heard myself praying the scriptures. As I continued praying, I began to feel a calmness come upon me. And as His peace enveloped me, this is what I heard in my spirit, "The rest of the content is for the book."

"Oh my goodness!" I gasped. I quickly sat up on the edge of my chair and paused, with both hands flat against my chest. I was stunned by what I heard. God had already been revealing to me that I was going to write a book. This was the final confirmation from Him that convinced me it was indeed His calling and not something I was making up in my head. I wiped my face, grabbed some paper, and created an outline for each speaking session. Those outlines are what helped me to narrow down what I shared at the retreat that weekend—and prepared me to write this book.

But God wasn't done. The next day at church, my pastor preached a sermon where almost everything he said was already written into parts of my message. I could barely stay in my seat that Sunday—I knew exactly what God was doing.

The day before, when I was crying and wanting to give up, I asked God if I was saying the right thing. I started doubting myself and wondering if the message was truly from Him. I believed He had written it on my heart, but the imposter syndrome caused me to stumble and doubt. He used my pastor the very next day to speak encouragement into my heart.

Don't allow the enemy to stop you from obeying God's call. The Bible tells us that we are not to have a spirit of fear.

"For the Spirit God gave us does not make us timid, but gives us power, love and self-discipline." (2 Timothy 1:7)

Perfection Is a Lie

There is a difference between having a spirit of fear and being afraid to do something but doing it anyway. Having a spirit of fear is living in fear and allowing it to paralyze you. A spirit of fear prevents you from obeying what God calls you to do. It causes you to procrastinate for long periods of time. Sometimes when you're living in a spirit of fear, you will perform activities related to the call but never move forward to actually finish the assignment. Extensive preparation and prolonged research are a couple of reasons why you remain in the planning or "not yet" stage. In the spirit of fear, you refuse to make a move until perfection is achieved.

Hear this one thing: perfection is a lie. It doesn't exist. Waiting until you reach perfection before starting what God has called you to do is futile. Seeking perfection in your obedience to God leaves no room for growth. Whenever God calls you to an assignment, His intention is for you to grow through the experience. Your faith is strengthened through obedience. Your relationship with Jesus grows deeper as you walk in His calling. You learn more about yourself in obedience to God. In contrast, the pursuit of perfection is a stressful, life-draining activity that usually prevents you from moving forward in obedience.

In my role as an online sewing instructor, I love teaching beginners the basics of garment construction. I'm very open with my community about my faith and I seek to conduct myself in a manner that represents Jesus well. I show up as myself and allow my personality to shine through because, in doing so, they are able to see my heart. And at the core of my heart is Jesus. When they can see the heart, they can experience the Light of my Savior.

When I launched my sewing YouTube channel, I started with a beginner's sewing course, walking the viewers through the process of making their own garments step by step, with very detailed instructions. As much as I tried to make that course perfect, I made mistakes and said things that still cause me to cringe when I think about it. The course was created in 2016, and people are still commenting on how much it helps them to learn to sew. There are other sewing tutorials on my channel where I've actually shared my mistakes and taught the viewers what to do should they encounter the same issues.

As I allowed myself to be true to who I am and put out the videos without being too hard on myself, not only were viewers able to learn how to sew, but many have commented on how much they appreciate my openness and courage to share my faith. The very first video in that course has over 700,000 views—and that's the video where I told people to purchase their fabric by the inches, when I meant to say yards. If I had taken those videos down because they weren't perfect, just imagine how many people would have missed out on content that helped them along their journey into sewing. Not only that, but I learned so much through the experience, and my videos have improved a great deal. You see how that works? Stop waiting for perfection. Just do what God calls you to do, working with what you have at the time, and allow yourself to grow and become better through the process. You've got this.

The enemy doesn't want you to shine the Light of Jesus through your obedience—so use the Word of God as your combat ammunition to fight off the lies and accusations. Then move forward in obedience to live in the Light as He is in the Light. Remember, the perfectionist mindset prevents you from moving forward. Everything you need to walk in obedience is already within you. You've been equipped for the call. Now, STEP into it.

Chapter 23

STEP into It

Never in my life would I have ever imagined that God would use the death of my husband to awaken me to a new way of thinking, a new way of living, a greater sense of purpose. Purpose doesn't change with life's circumstances or shift as we experience different seasons. It's foundational, and everything else should be carried out through that lens of purpose. Back in 2018, you couldn't have told me that I would be writing a book a few years later. As I write these words, I'm still in awe. I shake my head in wonder at God's grace, mercy, and power. How is it that the God I've served all these years chose to do this after the most devastating time of my life?

It's because that's what He does. It aligns with His character. He uses broken people for His glory. He shows His power through the works of those who choose to look up while walking through the valley. God always operates from a position of love and invites you to join in His kingdom work. Your obedience is an act of love in return.

When I first received the assignment to write this book, I thought to myself, "But I'm not an author." And in my spirit, I received the response, "God is the Author of your life. In obedience to Him, you will be who He says you are. He has called you to this assignment; therefore, you're writing under His authority. Be the author of His message planted on your heart through the experiences He's allowed in your life."

I knew that if I wanted to find myself healthy and whole on the other side of my grief journey, I would have to allow God to have His way through this process. In surrendering my doubts to His truth, I began to see the transformation taking place in my heart.

Overcoming through Transformation

Overcoming is important—and when you're in a trial, that's what you expect. However, overcoming, in and of itself, is not the end goal. Transformation, paired with overcoming, is what will help you to emerge from the trial a better person. As you use the principles and pillars I've outlined in this book, you can experience the transformation.

Looking ahead to the end result (overcoming) could produce anxiety and dread about timing. Living through the trial and embracing the four steps, however, builds character and strength. When you focus only on overcoming, you will miss the treasures and golden nuggets that are planted along the journey. The treasures are what you carry with you to the other side, allowing you to emerge with more than just the badge of being an overcomer—that leaves you the same coming out as you were going in. There's something greater about living through and thriving in the midst of the trial. Countless people overcome trials of all kinds. But not all walk out of it changed for the better. Allow yourself to be transformed.

Your transformation will look different than anyone else's. It will be unique to your design, to who God created you to be. It will serve those He has ordained to be encouraged and inspired through you. When He calls you to do something, the transformation continues as you carry out His assignment. You've been given authority to walk in His truth. The only thing that will keep you from obedience is yourself. And the only way you will step into it is by believing and simply moving forward. One day at a time. One step at a time. One breath at a time.

Believe

You've probably heard the saying, "You become what you believe." I understand this on a much deeper level now. I've shared how I had to work through my own limiting beliefs. The shift happened during the awakening, when I decided to believe that I could do what God told me to do. Because of my experiences, I'm a firm believer that you really do live what you believe. It has nothing to do with your financial or educational status. You could be the richest, most educated person in the world, but if you don't believe you can use your gifts to serve others and make an impact, you will not do it. Your wealth and knowledge don't guarantee that you will live a life that glorifies God. It is only by walking in obedience to His call that He is glorified through you.

A mediocre existence is the result of a mediocre mindset. Change your mindset, change your life. Thrive! Every word, every action, every destiny begins with a thought. You were created for something greater than mediocrity—so start believing it.

Let me dig into mediocrity a bit more, because I don't want you to believe that the state of mediocrity is the same for everyone. Whether or not you're living a mediocre life is dependent upon your choices and upon who God created you to be in Christ. For example, if He calls me to a certain assignment and I choose disobedience to stay in my comfort zone, I would call that mediocre living. Whenever God calls you to an assignment, it is for the purpose of spiritual growth. When you choose disobedience, you're choosing to remain stagnant.

It's also important to point out that what may be mediocre for one person could be a level-up for another. And what may be a level-up for me could very well be considered mediocre for you. This is why it's so important that we not compare ourselves with other people. Because each of us is uniquely designed by God, our individual calls will never look the same. Your level-up is not for me—God didn't give me your calling. If God calls me to an assignment and I look at your assignment and think to myself, "Well, they're doing something so awesome and I could never do that," I create a mediocre mindset that is sure to keep me in disobedience.

Stay focused on *your* calling. Don't allow yourself to get caught up in what others are doing, who they're serving, or how they're serving. Your calling is between you and God. When He calls you to an assignment, what another person is doing is none of your business.

When Jesus told Peter to "Feed my sheep," Peter said, "What about him, Lord?" referring to another disciple. Jesus said, "What is that to you? You must follow me" (John 21:15–22). Sometimes we're so focused on what others are doing or not doing that we can't see the vision God is giving us.

Focusing on others—their success, popularity, and appearance—is a sure way to keep you in a state of disobedience to God and mediocrity.

As a child of the Most High, you were created for excellence. God has chosen you to shine His Light into a world that needs Him. The only way for you to operate in excellence is by walking in obedience to His call on your life. It means moving forward with His plans, regardless of what anyone else is doing. That is excellence. But you must believe what He says about you.

Once you decide to believe what He says, your actions will follow. Pay close attention as God shows you more of Himself throughout the journey. As you see Him more clearly, you will see yourself, the self He created you to be. Once you have allowed the doubt and fear to fall away and BELIEVE, nothing will keep you from moving forward.

STEP into It

As I sit here, closing out the final chapter of my first book, I feel a sense of gratitude. I've gone back and forward about how to close. I told myself that the end needed to be really good, that I needed to go out with a bang. "Leave them gasping, Anita," I told myself. I wanted you to leave with your heart pounding, eager to apply the steps to your life. In my mind, success would mean you enjoyed the book, went out and told all your friends to read it, and shared it all over your social platforms. I've rewritten this ending so many times, but nothing felt quite right. It never felt authentic.

But as I sat down to make more changes to this final version, I received a message in my spirit—what I sometimes refer to as a spiritual download, a prompting from the Holy Spirit. I believe this one came because I was trying too hard to produce an outcome with the closing of the book. Ha! Can you believe that?

Here's the message I received: "The outcome is not your call."

Oh my goodness! It wasn't until I heard this truth that I realized what I was doing. I was trying to orchestrate that which belongs to the Lord. I was crafting something for a response, rather than allowing my heart to show up. And the Holy Spirit wouldn't let it be.

When it's not genuine, you just feel it.

I've already shared that whenever God calls you to an assignment, it is for the benefit of others. Your only responsibility is to say yes to the call and step into it. God does not hold you accountable for how people respond to your obedience. Before He even calls you to service, He orchestrates a community of people to be part of the journey.

So, why do I feel gratitude here at the end of this book? I'm grateful because I now realize that success isn't tied to what others think, say, or do. Success is being obedient to God's call. And the greatest outcome for me is the work He has done on my heart during this journey.

I'm still amazed that this book turned out to be for me first. God used this writing journey to further facilitate my healing process. He's increased my confidence in preparation for the next assignment. This act of obedience has carried over into other areas of my life. I'm a work in progress, and I know that the transformation will continue as God provides more opportunities for growth. I have been given the tools to STEP into obedience, and I hope you have captured them too while reading this book.

Through the trials of life, from the ashes of devastation, God gives you power to STEP into your purpose, which is to glorify Him, by walking in obedience to the call He's placed on your life.

The next time you come face to face with a life trial, allow God to do His work as you STAND in your faith, TRUST the sovereignty of God, ENDURE the trial with grace, and PROCEED to God's purpose.

"When you live in your DESIGN, it is from there that God SHINES!" You've got this! STEP into it!

"The Lord bless you and keep you; the Lord make his face shine upon you and be gracious to you; the Lord turn his face toward you and give you peace."

(Numbers 6:24–26)

Acknowledgments

With much gratitude, I'd like to thank the people who supported me along this journey, and those who have been instrumental in helping me to write and publish my first book.

First, I must give praise to God for calling me to this work. There had to be a call before the book.

To the Authors Who Lead team: Without your help, this book would not be. Thank you Azul and Steve for making me feel welcome when I first showed up at your Writer's Workshop. Thank you for coaching me through the writing process and helping to bring my book from an idea to publication.

To the incredible Authors Who Lead team who helped turn my manuscript into an amazing book: Emily, Kim, Valene, McKell, Lisa, Justin, and Kaitlin. It was a joy working with each of you. Your efficiency throughout this process made it an enjoyable experience.

To my sons, Brandon and Jordon, for believing that your mom could write a book. Thank you for cheering for me along the way and supporting me in telling my story. Your expressions of love and excitement throughout this process made my heart beat with joy.

Thank you to my mother and sister for going down memory lane with me to help me remember the events of my childhood. Thank you for encouraging me to tell my story.

Thank you to my church family, Desert Winds Community Church, for all you've done to support me along this journey of restoration. Thank you for believing in me, even at the lowest time of my life. You helped me to build a solid foundation and I will be forever grateful.

Acknowledgments

Thank you to the Los Angeles Fire Department for your incredible support of me and my sons during our time of greatest need. You will forever be a part of our family.

To my sewing community for walking alongside me virtually when I struggled to find my way back after tragedy. Thank you for waiting for me and lifting me up with your words of encouragement. You are part of the reason I will continue to STEP.

To all of my friends who have stood in agreement with me about writing this book. Thank you for seeing the potential in me to bring forth something that will help others to STEP into their purpose.

Abuse Hotlines

I found the following United States hotline phone numbers through a quick Google search. I am not affiliated with any of the organizations listed below. I have not researched or spoken with any of these agencies about the services they provide or method of operation. I am sharing the information in case there is anyone who may need help. Please call 911 if you are in danger and need immediate help.

If you live outside of the United States, you may find hotline phone numbers for your area through a Google search.

Domestic Abuse	1-800-799-7233
Sexual Abuse	1-800-656-4673
Suicide Prevention	1-800-273-8255
Sex Trafficking	1-888-373-7888
Elderly Abuse	1-800-799-7233
Substance Abuse	1-800-662-4357
Child Abuse	1-800-422-4453

1-YEAR
BIBLE READING PLAN

READ THE ENTIRE BIBLE IN ONE YEAR!

MONTHLY PLANS!   DAILY ASSIGNMENTS!   GUIDED READING!

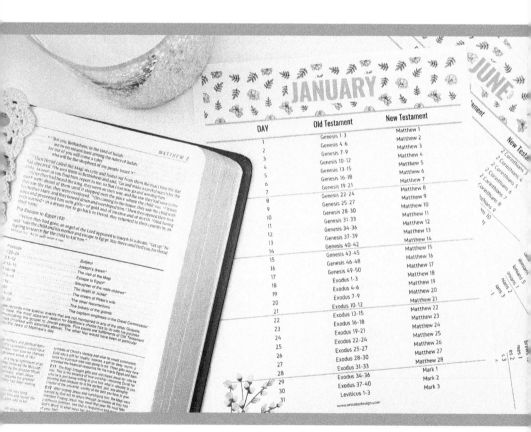

GET YOUR FREE 1-YEAR BIBLE READING PLAN

CHANGE BEGINS IN THE MIND

MINDSET SCRIPTURE CARDS

INTHIANS 10:5

h arguments and
at sets itself up ag
ie of God, and we
y thought to make
ent to Christ."

itabydesign.com

ROMANS 12:2

"Do not conform any longer to
pattern of this world, but b
transformed by the renewing
mind. Then you will be able to
approve what God's will is - h
pleasing and perfect w

www.anitabydesign.com

The Word of God Is Your Weapon against Negative Thinking and Limiting Beliefs

A set of 20 Bible Verses to assist you in memorizing Scripture.
CHANGE YOUR THINKING! CHANGE YOUR LIFE!

WWW.ANITABYDESIGN.COM/SCRIPTURE-CARDS

Contact Me

SPEAKING

HIRE ME FOR YOUR
NEXT WOMEN'S EVENT

WWW.ANITAMORRIS.ORG

SEWING

LEARN TO SEW FOR BEGINNERS

WWW.LEARNTOSEWCOURSE.COM

FOLLOW ME

✉ WWW.CONTACT@ANITABYDESIGN.COM
▶ WWW.YOUTUBE.COM/C/ANITABYDESIGN
📷 WWW.INSTAGRAM.COM/ANITABYDESIGN
𝓟 WWW.PINTEREST.COM/ANITABYDESIGN
🌐 WWW.ANITABYDESIGN.COM

INSPIRATION!

SPIRITUAL
DEVELOPMENT!

SEWING!

JOIN MY
COMMUNITY

ANITABYDESIGN.COM/JOIN-MY-COMMUNITY

About the Author

Anita Morris

Anita Morris is a woman of faith, mother of two sons, author, speaker, and creator of a popular DIY fashion brand. Anita understands the struggle that arises when one is faced with a devastating life trial, and she shares a message of hope, strength, and perseverance. She reaches women, all over the world, encouraging them to step into purpose, even in the midst of trials. She has served as keynote speaker at multiple women's events in Southern California. Anita says, "When you live according to the way you've been created, it is from that place that God will use you to bless other people." Her favorite things to do are garment sewing and tea parties. Visit Anita's website at https://www.anitabydesign.com.

If you enjoyed this book and found it helpful, please leave a REVIEW on Amazon.

Thank you!

Lightning Source UK Ltd.
Milton Keynes UK
UKHW052006050122
396669UK00011B/190